T0329013

AN ENGLISH SYLLABUS

AN ENGLISH SYLLABUS

BY

E. E. REYNOLDS

Author of *Exercises in English*, &c.
Editor of Marlowe's *Edward II*
&c.

CAMBRIDGE
AT THE UNIVERSITY PRESS
1931

CAMBRIDGE
UNIVERSITY PRESS

University Printing House, Cambridge CB2 8BS, United Kingdom

Cambridge University Press is part of the University of Cambridge.

It furthers the University's mission by disseminating knowledge in the pursuit of education, learning and research at the highest international levels of excellence.

www.cambridge.org
Information on this title: www.cambridge.org/9781316612712

© Cambridge University Press 1931

First published 1931
First paperback edition 2016

A catalogue record for this publication is available from the British Library

ISBN 978-1-316-61271-2 Paperback

To

THE MEMORY
of
ARNOLD SMITH
INSPIRED TEACHER
FRIEND

CONTENTS

PREFACE

The purpose of this book is to offer detailed suggestions for the planning of the English work in schools. Under present conditions much of the English teaching has to be done by those who are not specialists, or possibly by some who are not readers themselves. It is therefore important that there should be a carefully drawn-up scheme of work so that each teacher concerned can see exactly what he has to do and how his part dovetails into the whole.

The syllabus and the suggestions on method are based on some years of experience in teaching in Secondary Schools, and it may be claimed that, whatever the shortcomings of the scheme may be, it is a practicable syllabus, and frankly faces the exigencies of time-tables and of examinations. This has sometimes meant the sacrifice of ideals for the sake of expediency, but as so much depends on the success of pupils in the School Certificate Examination, it is clearly a duty to frame our scheme to satisfy the conditions under which the work has to be done. We may deplore the fact that employers put so much stress on the result of that examination, and that it hangs like a thunder-cloud over the schools, but until the world of business changes its mind, we have to meet its demands for the sake of the pupils' futures.

I hope that not too much has been lost in the process of organising the scheme. Any syllabus written down on paper looks a cold-blooded affair, and may well dismay the enthusiast; but there is indeed little rigidity in the

scheme here suggested, with the exception of those sections dealing with grammar. I have tried to give a number
of ideas on how to treat books without killing them, how
to use poetry in the class-room without robbing it of its
beauty, and how to make the writing of English an
adventure for all.

The enthusiast will rightly go his own way. Ernest
Raymond's portrait of Elam in *Through Literature to Life*
shows the real teacher, or rather inspirer, of English doing
his work of passing on his own passion for all that is good
in our language. 'I don't care twopence about giving you
facts—anybody can give you *facts*—the official in the next
class-room can do *that*—and anybody can remember facts.
I'm going to give you ideas. I don't think it matters much
if ideas are right, so long as they are ideas—so long as you
think and *feel*. I don't want to teach you to *know*, but to
interpret. See?' Happy the school that has such a man on
its Staff, and fortunate indeed the pupils he enthuses. For
the others, especially for those who have to take their own
Forms in English, guidance is helpful.

I hope this syllabus at least demonstrates that even
with examinations looming ahead, there is great latitude
and scope for the personal enthusiasms of the teacher, and
for using to their full those methods that have made the
teaching of English during the last twenty years humane
instead of inhumane, as much of it was at the beginning
of this century.

As my experience has been entirely with boys, I have
naturally had them in mind while writing this book, but
I hope it will also prove of help in girls' schools. For this
reason the word 'pupil' has been used, but the awkward-
ness of 'he' or 'she' has been avoided.

Some of the material has appeared previously in *The Nineteenth Century and After*, *The Times Educational Supplement*, or *The Journal of Education*, and my thanks are due to the editors for permission to make use of my contributions to their pages.

E. E. R.

August, 1931

There is a useful art of Grammar, which takes for its province the right and the wrong in speech. Style deals only with what is permissible to all, and even revokes, on occasion, the rigid laws of Grammar or countenances offences against them. Yet no one is a better judge of equity for ignorance of the law, and grammatical practice offers a fair field wherein to acquire ease, accuracy, and versatility. The formation of sentences, the sequence of verbs, the marshalling of the ranks of auxiliaries are all, in a sense, to be learned. There is a kind of inarticulate disorder to which writers are liable, quite distinct from a bad style, and caused chiefly by lack of exercise. An unpractised writer will sometimes send a beautiful and powerful phrase jostling along in the midst of a clumsy sentence—like a crowned king escorted by a mob.

But Style cannot be taught. Imitation of the masters, or of some one chosen master, and the constant purging of language by a severe criticism, have their uses, not to be belittled; they have also their dangers. The greater part of what is called the teaching of style must always be negative, bad habits may be broken down, old malpractices prohibited. The pillory and the stocks are hardly educational agents, but they make it easier for honest men to enjoy their own....

All style is gesture, the gesture of the mind and of the soul. Mind we have in common, inasmuch as the laws of right reason are not different for different minds. Therefore clearness and arrangement can be taught, sheer incompetence in the art of expression can be partly remedied. But who shall impose laws upon the soul?

From *Style*, by Sir Walter Raleigh
(London: Edward Arnold & Co.), by permission

GENERAL PRINCIPLES

When a pupil leaves school he should be able to speak correctly and pleasantly, to write clear, plain English, to read with understanding, and to enjoy his heritage of a great Literature. To accomplish such a wide purpose it is essential that the English work of the school should be carefully planned as a whole, so that throughout proper attention may be given to speaking, reading and writing.

I. SPEAKING

Our purpose is not to train all people to speak with exactly similar accents, but to make sure that our pupils when they leave us can speak in such a way that no ear can be offended by ugly sounds. It is impossible to define scientifically what is meant by 'a good accent', but we can all recognise it when we hear it. The English teacher's first business is to make certain that he himself uses this good accent, for his manner of speaking will have more effect on his pupils than anything else. They hear him in class when he speaks to them, and when he reads to them; they hear him out of class, on the playing-field and in the school. The fatal thing would be for him to use one accent in English lessons and another in the corridor. Constant watchfulness will be necessary, and training to overcome any defects once the teacher has learnt to recognise his own shortcomings.

This is not the place to attempt even a cursory treatment of the subject of speech-training; there are ways and means of getting such training open to all teachers if they have not already had it; there are courses of lectures and practices during vacations; there are many good books on the subject (see p. 102). The point to bear in mind is that every teacher of English will derive benefit from such training, and the more nearly he approaches an accepted accent in his own speech, the more quickly will his pupils learn to speak clearly and pleasantly.

The value of phonetics in English is still a matter of dispute. Where phonetics are used in other language classes, it is clearly desirable that the same should be done in English. If the teacher himself feels that the use of phonetics would be a real aid to improving the speech of his pupils, he should certainly give them the necessary training, but this should come as early as possible in the school course. No provision has been made in this syllabus for teaching phonetics because so much of the work in the early stages has to be done by those who have had no special training.

Much, however, can be done to correct defects of speech if the teacher has even an elementary knowledge of how the sounds of the language are made, and this modicum of knowledge should certainly be acquired by all; it can be gained by means of a text-book and a looking-glass.

During all lessons the teacher must keep his ears alert for ugly and undesirable sounds; no attempt should be made during the actual speaking or reading of the pupil to correct defects, as interruptions of this kind defeat their own purpose by making the pupil self-conscious. It is better to make a note of bad pronunciation and later in private to help the pupil to improve. Jingles and other special sentences will be found useful exercises to suggest to the pupil for private practice. Grammatical mistakes should be corrected as soon as the pupil has finished what he is saying. The teacher should keep a note of these to make sure that they are corrected in time and not constantly repeated. The pupil should also note such errors down in his note-book as a reminder. Nagging, or ridiculing peculiarities of speech, must be avoided; patience and sympathy will achieve most.

The task of improving pronunciation is not an easy one; the teacher is at odds sometimes with the home surroundings; he has to compete with the americanisation of accent resulting by frequent attendance at the 'Talkies';

the accent of the B.B.C. announcer often suggests an artificial standard; if the school is situated in an industrial town, there may be the added conflict of the speech of the street. Even if all these difficulties are present at the same time he can at least hope to do one thing: to set a standard of accent in his own speech that will be a counteracting influence. Any attempt, however, to reproduce an artificial accent which is supposed to be a mark of culture should be severely suppressed. Many a teacher has experienced the shock of meeting an old pupil who has acquired a way of speech that does not ring true. We do not want mannered speech, but honest English.

In addition to his talk in the normal course of his work, the teacher should give particular care to the reading aloud of stories, verse and of prose extracts to the class. His aim should be to widen the acquaintance of the pupils with bookland, to stimulate their interests in different authors and subjects, and, above all, by the verve with which he reads, to show that a delight in reading is not an academic fiction, but a real experience. He must communicate his own enthusiasms and so awaken the curiosity of his hearers. For this reason, apart from what is read from class books, the teacher should frequently read aloud what has captured his own fancy; it is difficult to pass on the pleasures of a book that does not interest ourselves. He should not be too bothered about reading only such matter as he thinks the pupils can understand; it is good for them to hear occasionally passages that will call for close attention, or passages that will appeal to the ear by the beauty of rhythm. All Literature is open for our use, and if we want to let our pupils know something of the variety of pleasures that await them we must choose our readings from a wide field.

Oral work should play a large part in the early years of the Course; suggestions for this will be found in the syllabus. It is often forgotten that every spoken word in the class is either an aid or a hindrance to the improvement of English; a good standard of speaking should always be insisted upon. This to a certain degree applies to all the schoolwork, but it is the particular business of the English teacher to see that slipshod ways of talking and of answering questions are not encouraged during his own periods. This does not imply the encouragement of a stilted manner of expression, but it does mean clearness of diction and of meaning, as well as clearness of enunciation. The earlier the habit of good speaking is developed, the easier will be the later years of training.

Care must be taken to see that each pupil gets a share in the oral work. There will always be those who are fond of hearing themselves and to whom the spoken word comes with facility. Others are more retiring, and perhaps one of the difficulties of this work is to draw them out of that retirement, and to persuade them to express their thoughts as freely as their fellows. Considerable skill is needed to achieve this and at the same time to avoid the deadening monotony of answering round the class in turn. Dramatic work provides the best opportunity of giving practice to all in speaking; the reading of verse and of passages of prose selected by the pupils are other opportunities for encouraging a good accent. Questions on what has been read, general conversation on school and other topics, and the various ways suggested in the syllabus should all be called into service.

The teaching of grammar offers many opportunities for useful oral questioning and answering. This is not the place to enter into a discussion on the question of the place that grammar should take in the curriculum. As a matter of expediency it is important that grammar should be taught carefully and thoroughly, and that the bulk of it should be done between the ages of 11 and 14. In Preparatory Schools where Latin is sometimes begun at an early age, it will be necessary to teach the elements of grammar at the same time. Provision is made for this in Stage I of the syllabus, but it is better to avoid the subject if possible until the age of 11. If the study of grammar is left until later it will occupy time that can more usefully be spent in reading, and it will then be too late to be of value in the learning of other languages. The syllabus here given is full so that the building up of knowledge may be done systematically. The study begins with the sentence and gradually the functions of the various parts of speech are explained. Considerable emphasis has been put upon structure of complex sentences and their nature, as this is particularly valuable both for English and other languages.

The teacher should always pick out, from other language text-books used by the pupils, parallel examples to those used for the English lesson, so that there may be co-ordination of the grammar work throughout the teaching of languages in the school. It is essential that for this purpose the same terminology should be used in all language work. Pupils have been too often befogged by hearing one set of terms used in the English lessons, another in French and possibly a third in Latin. It might almost be said that it does not much matter what terminology is adopted as long as it is used systematically throughout the school. In this syllabus alternative terms have been purposely used to meet as many requirements as possible. It is most important that the English and language teachers in a school should meet together and come to some decision on this essential matter. The difficulties are considerable, as a desirable text-book from one point of view may be undesirable from another. Fortunately the report of the Joint Committee on Grammatical Terminology has been widely accepted by recent writers of text-books, though each author may introduce some small variation and thereby rob the scheme of its greatest value.

It will be found in experience that nearly all the grammar work suggested can be done orally, and this method is to be preferred to written work, as the teacher can then be certain that important facts are understood, and mistakes can be immediately rectified. Whole periods devoted to the subject should be avoided; an occasional one may be necessary, such as when the meaning of clause has to be explained; but generally ten minutes at a time will be sufficient to cover the syllabus with ease.

A text-book is not necessary in the teaching of grammar. It is far better that all explanation should come from the teacher. Too often the fullness of the grammar book confuses the pupil. All that is needed is a book of examples and questions. The ordinary text-book does not, for reasons of space, give enough examples and exercises, and in grammar teaching quantity is important. My own *Exercises in English* and *Intermediate Exercises in English* are designed to meet the need for a large stock of questions for oral practice.

II. READING

The choice of books for each class is an important matter. We want to train the pupils in how to read a book, and at the same time lay the foundations of good taste in reading. It is an old gibe at schoolmasters that they kill any interest in Literature when a book becomes a text-book. There has been in the past reason for this statement. Books that were available in cheap form were not numerous and consequently one book had to last a year. Some of us can remember grinding at one of Scott's novels week after week for three terms; it has needed a strong liking for books to survive such treatment. There was also an idea that books were to be used as specimens for the study of etymology, grammar, allusions and indeed anything other than as Literature.

It may be safely stated that such methods are no longer favoured. Publishers have now produced a wealth of material for our use in schools. The old style of text had an institutional appearance with its cheap binding and poor print. English texts are now a delight to handle. This in itself does much to foster a greater respect for Literature. The range of titles is also wide enough to meet all tastes; the old favourites are there, but we can now use, if we will, stories by Conrad, Buchan, Tolstoy, and other modern writers; or there are collections of one-act plays, books of nature observation by Fabre and Hudson, and accounts of their journeys by the great explorers. The literatures of all countries are being laid under contribution for the delight of the modern schoolboy. The teacher's difficulty now has become one of selecting suitable material from this wealth.

The first consideration must be the age of the pupils for whom the books are intended. We often, however, underrate the capacity of our pupils and tend to give them books which do not call for any effort on their part. In the syllabus a few titles have been suggested under each year; these are merely guides to the type of book that has proved successful for the varying ages. Not many modern books have been included.

Some seem to think that to include modern books is a sign of being up-to-date in methods; but it is part of the teacher's function to introduce the pupils to that tradition of Literature on which all sound modern work must be based. It is therefore important that established classics should play a large part in the school reading: judicious selection is necessary. Much of the disfavour shown for the older writers is due to unwise choice for school reading. Bacon's *Essays* for example is not suitable for young pupils, and has a doubtful value even for the seniors.

The books in this syllabus have been chosen mainly because they offer the right kind of work for each stage. Thus in the early years considerable dramatic work should be done, so books have been chosen that will supply material for this.

At least three prose books should be read each year; this is a workable number and prevents too much intensive reading, a danger we must all guard against. The right use of the books is more important than the choice in many ways. Bad methods will ruin a good book. We should aim at passing on to the pupil the pleasures of reading. For this reason much of the reading can be done silently either in school or at home. Reading round the class serves no useful purpose at any stage of the work; once a pupil has done his bit, he generally day-dreams; he becomes passive and not active. Reading aloud should certainly be done, but the pupils should be encouraged to select what they shall read from any books they like. This will introduce an element of suspense into the work that will maintain a lively interest, as each pupil will listen for what his fellows have chosen, and mentally assess it as either good or dull. This method has the advantage of widening the scope of reading; pupils will be brought into touch with books that otherwise would not come into the work.

As the pupils get older so the amount of reading aloud by them should decrease and silent reading increase. Much of the later work will be directional reading; a number of questions and problems are set on each book as a guide to important matters, and as a means of securing concentration. Examples of such questions will be found for the fourth year, on Thackeray's *English Humourists*.

There is the ever-present danger that we may give pupils the impression that there are two sorts of books, those read in school (therefore 'dry'), and those read out of school. This can be guarded against partly by wise choice of book for school reading, partly by having a varied selection in the school and class libraries, and also by the teacher getting to know at first-hand the books that are read for pleasure when the pupil's choice is unfettered. Lists are published from time to time by Public Libraries of the most popular books read in the Juvenile Departments; these lists should be studied carefully, and if the teacher is unacquainted with any of the authors mentioned, he should read their books in order to see what it is that interests the rising generation. In addition there is the whole field of cheap literature beloved of children of the ages of 13 and 14. It has become a habit with some teachers to pounce on 'bloods' (no longer penny but fourpenny), confiscate them and tell the victim that he should read 'decent' English. Such an attitude shows a lamentable ignorance of present-day 'bloods'. No English teacher has any right to condemn (or praise) books that he has not read himself, and if he would only read a few of these 'fourpennies' occasionally he would learn much about the interests of his pupils, and realise that the English is certainly as good as that of most of the seven-and-sixpenny novels he himself reads without worrying about their effect on *his* English! (Let him also read *Saxo Grammaticus: First Aid for the Best-Seller*, by Ernest Weekley.) This may not be to claim a high standard, but it is an efficient one. There is in these 'bloods' usually no waste of words, the meaning is clear, and the story is told in a workmanlike fashion. These are all qualities we should like to see in the compositions our pupils write. The following is a good sample of such writing:

Shortly after midnight the main steam pipe of the port engine burst, filling the engine-room with clouds of scalding vapour.

In accidents of this sort the sole chance of escape for the surviving engineers on duty was for them to throw themselves flat until the worst of the death-dealing blast of steam had exhausted itself.

Unfortunately the explosion also fractured the main oil fuel supply, and either an overturned oil-lamp or else a 'short' in one of the electric leads did the rest. A gust of oil ignited, and then ensued a battle between fire and the fire-quenching properties of steam. The fire, originated low down in the engine-room, gained the mastery and soon both engine and boiler rooms were a raging inferno.

The few survivors from this part of the ship had to abandon their posts. The starboard engine continued to function, and by aid of this help Captain Stopford was able to keep the ship stern on to the wind, thus giving the breeze less chance to fan the flames.

It was a forlorn task. Soon the starboard propeller ceased to revolve and the ship, losing way, drifted broadside-on in the trough of the sea.

Teachers who read some of these 'bloods' will meet old friends of their own youth: Sexton Blake and Nipper with their bloodhound are ageless, and Greyfriars School still flourishes.

I have dwelt upon this topic at some length because it does illustrate one or two important principles in the teaching of English. The teacher should be familiar with the books that the pupils like so that he can understand their preferences and find that common ground on which teacher and pupil must stand if there is to be that sympathy that is the basis of successful schoolwork. It is of even greater importance that the teacher should not be a hypocrite. By all means let him condemn 'bloods' if he knows what he is talking about and can give chapter and verse for his opinions, and be ready to discuss the matter on equal terms with the pupils; but to rate all such reading as rubbish, without knowing anything about it at first-hand, is foolish. He not only loses a means of looking into the boy mind, but he will rouse opposition, and the pupils will suspect that if he talks nonsense about what they know, he is probably talking nonsense about what they do not know.

Sincerity is of first importance in the teaching of English, and particularly in this matter of reading. It is fatal for the teacher to pretend that he likes what he doesn't, or that he habitually reads the 'classics' for his pleasure and by choice. Such lip-homage is soon detected by the pupils, and any chance he may have of influencing them will vanish at once. The ideal English teacher should be a reader, and passionately fond of Literature. Such men are comparatively rare in schools; when there is such a man on the Staff he should be allowed complete freedom of syllabus, books and methods —though, under present conditions, it would be well to give someone else charge of the Certificate Class. Others who have to take English periods should be scrupulously honest in the statement of their likes and dislikes. They may even take up such an attitude as, 'Well, I don't care for this book much myself, but those who are keen say we should read it. So let's see what we can get out of it'. That is at least an honest way of dealing with the subject, and will call out sympathy from the class; teacher and pupils then become explorers, trying to find out what it is that makes the particular book a fine one in the opinion of those who read. Both may discover new lines of interest and have their appreciation of Literature quickened.

So far I have been dealing with books as Literature. It is also important that we should teach pupils how to use books in the ordinary purposes of life. Books are read for instruction, for propaganda, and for supplying useful information. We should teach our pupils how to read such books and get out of them their best value, and also how to find information they want. It is pitiful to see week by week in some periodicals requests for information that could be obtained in any decent reference library if only the enquirers knew where to look. Anyone who has been through a full school course should at least know something of the use of books; one reason why few people have this knowledge is that they acquired the habit at school of relying on the teacher all the time, and not on the use of the school library or local reference library.

The syllabus suggests two ways in which this weakness can be corrected: in the third year a beginning is made with instruction in note-making, and also in the use of reference books. A further development is put down for the post-certificate years; the teaching of the principles of valid reasoning, and of scientific method. If such instruction is carried out, the pupils should leave school with a knowledge of how to use books, and also with the ability of judging the soundness of an argument. They will then be less prone than the present generation to accept the printed word at its face value.

Drama has an important place throughout the school English work. The 'play-way' has proved most productive in the teaching of younger pupils; as they get older so the appeal of the drama proper increases, and provided the play is treated as a play and not as something else, most valuable results can be obtained. Speaking becomes of first importance, understanding of meaning is necessary, and the imagination is stimulated.

Perhaps in the past too much stress has been laid on the plays of Shakespeare, and sometimes they have been included in the reading of the lower Forms. His plays should certainly be read in schools in spite of Mr George

Bernard Shaw's proscription. When he was asked for permission to include the second scene of *St Joan* in a schoolbook, he replied,

No. I lay my eternal curse on whomsoever shall now or at any time hereafter make schoolbooks of my works, and make me hated as Shakespeare is hated. My plays were not designed as instruments of torture.

Mr Shaw has in mind the methods of reading Shakespeare that were in vogue many years ago, though I have heard that here and there the plays are still used as mines of etymological and other irrelevant information. It may be safely stated that pupils now look forward to the periods when they read and act plays, and no longer dread them as some of us did in our schooldays.

No doubt the best method of using any play is to act it. If the pupils have been accustomed during their first two years to making up short scenes of their own, based on history or story, they will find little to puzzle them when confronted with Shakespeare in their third year. To enjoy the reading there must have been some groundwork to cultivate the dramatic attitude in which the imagination can picture scenes and visualise the characters. It is a pity to attempt this early dramatic training by means of simple plays specially written for the young. Most of these are poor material, and they rob the pupils of the valuable work of employing their own imaginations in building up scenes for themselves.

All Shakespeare's plays are not suitable for schools; in the syllabus suggestions are made for plays for each year; they will make varied appeals, and this is desirable so that each pupil may have an opportunity of reading a play that strongly attracts him.

For use in junior classes editions without notes, apart from modern equivalents of Elizabethan words, are most desirable, and can now be obtained in many different forms. Expurgation is necessary; the tastes of those days were coarser than ours, and for all the fun that is made of Thomas Bowdler, he did a good service, carried too far perhaps, when he made the plays readable without offence. But expurgation is not sufficient for the first year of use; there must be a shortening of the texts and a deletion of difficult passages. Scholars may shudder at such a suggestion, but if they were to have actual experience in using the plays in school, they, too, would probably agree that judicious cutting is needed to make the plays more palatable to immature taste. Such a difficult passage as Scene vii of the second Act of *As You Like It*, lines 70 to 87: 'Why, who cries out on pride', may be a stumblingblock in a scene that moves forward quite easily without it.

It is important that in the fourth year (the second of Shakespeare reading) an idea should be given to the class of the structure of the Elizabethan playhouse. If possible a rough model of one should be constructed by some of the pupils in the school workshop. With this for illustration, much can be made clear in the plays that otherwise would be difficult to realise.

The syllabus gives full suggestions for using the plays at various stages. All is pleasant work until the Certificate year arrives; then more intensive work has to be done to meet examination requirements, but even then the play-method will be found the most productive. The trouble is that there is no certainty as to the lines on which the examination paper will be set; the questions set usually of recent years have certainly been more reasonable than of old, but occasionally an odd question is asked that suggests a wrong attitude to the reading of plays in school. Where possible it is better to avoid taking a play if the alternative is a prose text that will benefit by intensive study.

It is a pity to limit play-reading to the works of Shakespeare. Many plays by his contemporaries are readable, and there are also the plays of Sheridan, Goldsmith and of the modern writers. One-act plays are well worth reading, and these are now obtainable in various inexpensive editions. If possible a performance of plays should be given in front of the whole school. The prospect of facing a real audience has the power of tightening up interest and producing the best of which the pupils are capable. In such school performances it is not desirable that the players should be word perfect where they have principal parts; provided the words are very familiar, the book can be carried on the stage.

The possibility of taking the pupils to public productions of the plays should be investigated. There is no point in these being limited to those that they happen to be reading at the time. Shakespearean performances are too rare to miss.

It would be superfluous for me to urge the need for using the Bible as Literature throughout the school. There are now available a number of editions suitable for reading in class which avoid the clumsiness of verse and of chapter divisions. We have perhaps in the past too frequently neglected the reading of the Bible, perhaps because, unhappily, we have had to tread so delicately in our treatment of religious instruction. One result of this has undoubtedly been the misuse of the Bible; the 'Scripture' lesson has too often meant perfunctory reading round the class with occasional remarks of a non-committal character from the teacher. From the literary point of view alone, we have here an ancient literature in a matchless translation, that can set a standard of beautiful language unequalled in appeal, if only we will allow it to make that appeal.

In the highest classes a series of lessons on the literary character of the Bible would be of great value, and would do much to stimulate the study of one of the great influences on English speech during the last three hundred years, an influence that unfortunately has tended to decrease with the vast output of popular novels.

A word should be said about the use of books of selections. It is desirable that as a rule complete books should be read in preference to abridgments. But the prose anthology, or book of selections, has an important place in teaching, provided the selections are of reasonable length and not snippets. A pupil may be introduced in this way to fresh reading while at the same time getting an idea of the variety of styles and treatments that our Literature offers. The detailed study of a fine passage, the *lecture expliquée*, is a method that has proved of great value. If, however, the teacher follows the recommendation of frequently reading aloud this will serve some of the purposes of a printed book of selections. Collections of complete letters, of essays and of short stories are hardly to be considered in this category, and they are suggested in the lists of books given.

Abridgments are generally to be avoided unless the teacher is quite certain that their use may stimulate the pupils to go to the complete book afterwards. Before adopting such an abridgment, the teacher should carefully compare it with the original to make sure that the true value of the original has not been entirely lost.

Re-tellings of myths, of older writers such as Froissart and Chaucer may be legitimately used in the younger classes as material for dramatisation, but should never be used with older pupils as substitutes for the originals.

No other form of Literature calls for such delicate handling in school as poetry. A teacher who cannot feel its appeal can do untold harm by trying to 'teach' it as if the subject were like Mathematics or History with a definite and knowable content. In the past many have been given a lasting distaste for poetry by having suffered at the hands of such an uninspiring teacher. Some of us can remember analysing passages of great beauty, or having had to read and re-read the same poem week after week. It is to be hoped that such inhuman exercises are things of the past; paraphrase and analysis can be easily confined to verse of a pedestrian character, or to passages where meaning is as important as expression. Unfortunately examiners set for study such things of beauty as the odes of Keats, and then it is difficult to avoid 'murdering to dissect'. It is to be fervently hoped that poetry will be taken out of the examination syllabus as soon as possible: meantime teachers are advised to choose prose in preference to poetry when they select set books. It is with a sense of desecration that I have included in the syllabus some suggestions for treating set poetry: I can only hope that the methods outlined will indicate how to do the least harm.

The approach to poetry for the younger pupils comes naturally by way of the ballad and the story. This does not imply that these forms only should be used with them. In his Preface to *The Chilswell Book of Poetry*, Robert Bridges quotes with approval a few sentences in which Anatole France tells his own early experience.

In this little poem there were many phrases that were new to me, and which I could not understand; but the general effect of them seemed to me so sad and so beautiful that I was thrilled by a feeling that I had never known before—the charm of melancholy was revealed to me by a score of verses the literal meaning of which I could not have explained. The fact is that unless one has grown old, one does not need to understand deeply: things dimly comprehended can be quite touching, and it is very true that what is vague and indefinite has a charm for youth.

The late Laureate points out that it has been a mistaken idea to select for the young so-called simple poems, or those specially composed for them 'in a technique often as inept as their sentiment'. 'This mistake rested on two shallow delusions; first, that beauty must needs be fully apprehended before it can be felt or admired: secondly, that the young are unimaginative.'

Two principles should be observed in the use of poetry in the class-room. The appeal should primarily come through the ear. This implies that the teacher must be able to read poetry with delight to himself and to his hearers. The ability to do this is not a gift; to those who have a natural pleasure in verse, it comes with very little trouble; but others must train themselves to read poetry aloud in such a way that the music is heard; the two extremes to avoid are exaggeration of rhythm, and prosaicness of delivery. The second principle is that poetry should be read in bulk and not in snippets. A glance at the syllabus will show that each class is expected to read a considerable amount of poetry. Some may feel, for instance, that the number of poems put down to be read from the *Golden Treasury* during each lesson is excessive. It would be so if each poem had to be picked to pieces and used as the basis for exposition; but that is not intended. A few comments may be called for by the pupils themselves, or there may be occasions when some elucidation is needed, but the time spent on these matters should be far less than that spent in reading aloud, or in reading silently. The desultory reading of poetry should be encouraged, and the class library should contain many volumes of verse, and of anthologies, so that each pupil may browse at will and find the kind of poetry that appeals to him.

In the early years very little formal teaching should be given on such matters as rhyme, rhythm, forms of verse, figures of speech, etc. Later in the syllabus provision is made for this, but even then the teaching should be as informal as possible and arise out of what has been read beforehand.

It is doubtful if the writing of 'appreciations' has great value; the method certainly has dangers; it is comparatively easy to pick up a system of examining similes, metaphors, rhyme schemes and so on; it is so hard to get to the heart of things. Could we ourselves write an appreciation of a poem that has captured our spirit, and haunts us with its beauty? To ask children to achieve a task from which we ourselves shrink is not honest. There is a passage in Geoffrey Winthrop Young's *On High Hills* that can be applied to the child's appreciation of poetry.

It was not the *beauty* of hills which exaggerated for me their importance: that came far later. Only prodigious children see beauty in a composite 'view'. Startling single colours impress a child; very rarely form; never, honestly said, the relations of lines or of lines to colours, although the propriety of a child will echo its elders' enthusiasm self-deceivingly and often most convincingly. It was the *fact* of hills, their provoking mystery, and the excitement of their wilfulness in trying to go up where everything else was content to lie along.... Only very gradually, as the eye began to see lines and details in their relation to a general form, did hills take on personalities.

We must take heed in using poetry in schools that the teacher's enthusiasm is not merely echoed by the child 'self-deceivingly and often most convincingly'.

It is desirable that pupils should learn some poetry, but as far as possible they should be allowed to choose freely what they shall commit to memory. In the third and fourth years a few poems have been suggested as suitable for learning by heart; a knowledge of them should provide a standard of excellence for the pupils in their further reading; but even here this should not be too rigidly enforced if there are any signs that the selected poems do not meet with ready acceptance.

III. WRITING

'The style of a writer', said Goethe to Eckermann, 'is a faithful representative of his mind; therefore, if any man wish to write a clear style, let him be first clear in his thoughts: and if any would write in a noble style, let him first possess a noble soul.' Much has been written on the subject of style, but the heart of the matter has been put in this saying.

The business of a teacher of English is not to produce writers of purple passages, but to teach his pupils how to express their thoughts clearly. The important principle to grasp is that clear thinking *must* come before clear writing. The application of this to schoolwork lies in the necessity for setting exercises and subjects suited to the varying ages and experiences of the pupils. The formal essays of an older generation were too frequently on subjects of an abstract nature which could not possibly have corresponded to the content of the pupil's mind. No boy should be asked to write, for instance, on such a subject as 'Character'; he has neither the experience of life, nor the ability to think abstractly that is required to produce an honest piece of writing. Such essays were written in their hundreds, but they were mere collections of bits picked out of books, ill-assorted and undigested. (How useful Emerson was in those days! Lubbock's books, *The Use of Life*, etc., were also mines of material.)

Suggestions are made in the syllabus for suitable subjects at all stages. In the early years stress is laid on the need for much oral work as the basis for later written composition. As the interests of the pupils widen, so the subjects can become more varied. It should not be regarded as necessary or even desirable for all the pupils to be writing on the same subject at the same time. They should be allowed a choice of topic, and also of form of composition. Care must however be taken to ensure that each pupil gets practice in the different types of writing. In the early years there should be considerable practice in letter writing; other forms useful at this time are the diary, the story, the fable, the anecdote, the speech, and the dialogue. In the fourth year attention should be directed to the major forms, description, narrative, exposition and argument. At this stage more careful consideration should be given to structure, to the arrangement of ideas, and to proportion.

The answering of questions is another form of writing that should be practised. If instruction is given in this from the third year, much time and labour will be saved when examinations loom in sight. Many other exercises are aids to good writing; vocabulary work, paraphrase, précis, and note-making, all help to stress the need for clarity and order. The greatest appeal should, however, be made through the imagination; formal exercises seldom call out the best work, but the attempt to write a story or a dialogue stimulates the writer to do his best.

A note is necessary on the subject of marking. No teacher can possibly read thoroughly all the written work his pupils will have to do; he should practise the art of skimming if he is to keep his mind fresh and alert. There is no value in noting every mistake in a piece of written work, as the more comments made, the less likely is the pupil to give heed to them. It is a good scheme to fix on one main object in reading each piece of work; sometimes the nature of the subject will suggest the most important aspect of the writing to watch. At one time it may be arrangement that calls for most care, at another, punctuation.

In the fourth and fifth years it is advisable to read thoroughly two or three pieces of work each term. For this purpose some scheme for indicating the nature of the mistake or weakness will be necessary, as the whole value of marking is that the actual correction should be done by the pupil and not by the teacher. Such a scheme as the following has proved adequate.

	MEANING	METHOD OF CORRECTION
S	Spelling error	Write word correctly 5 times
P	Faulty punctuation	Write out sentence correctly punctuated
W	Wrong word used	Consult dictionary and write correct word in margin
§	Badly paragraphed	Indicate by brackets where paragraphs should begin
O	Something omitted	Supply word in margin
M	Meaning not clearly expressed	Re-write part underlined in clear English
G	Grammatical mistake, such as: concord, case of relative, use of tenses, form of word, etc.	Re-write sentence
R	Unnecessary repetition of wording or ideas	Re-write sentence
XX	Work not up to standard; this may apply to lack of thought in planning, or to bad handwriting, etc.	Re-write the whole piece

The teacher should be particularly careful to avoid asking for too great a quantity of written work. This applies not only to the total amount done each term, but to the actual length of each piece of composition. If the result is to be satisfactory, much time must be given to thinking out the subject and to getting the matter into shape; the actual writing is the final stage; too often teachers forget the time taken by the preliminary stages, and are unreasonably annoyed when they find that the results show no sign of careful preparation; a more modest quantity will often produce a better piece of work. A useful plan is to allow time in class for preparing the material for the essay, and then to leave the actual writing-out as homework.

There is an intimate connexion between reading and writing. The pupil who takes pleasure in reading will probably, though not always, write with more facility than one who reads little in his leisure time. If, therefore, the teacher can encourage his pupils to read more, he can expect an improvement in the written work they do for him.

THE SYLLABUS

GENERAL ARRANGEMENT

Stage	Description		Age range (years)
I	Preliminary		9–11
II	First year		11–12
III	Second year	*School*	12–13
IV	Third year	*Certificate*	13–14
V	Fourth year	*Course*	14–15
VI	Fifth year		15–16
VII	Advanced		16–18

The age ranges suggested are only rough guides, and assume average intelligence; an exceptional pupil of 13 might be able to do, for instance, Stage V.

This scheme can be adapted to suit various school conditions in the following way:

Type	Age range	Stages
*Primary School Preparatory School	9–14	I–III
*Modern (Central School)	11–16	II–VI
*Grammar (Secondary School)	11–18	II–VII
Public School	14–18	IV–VII

* Nomenclature of 'Hadow' Reports, 1926 and 1931.

Stage II recapitulates some of the work done in Stage I; as far as possible, however, the approach and treatment have been varied. In Preparatory Schools where Stage I has been thoroughly covered, it will be possible to omit some details given in Stage II for the purpose of supplying a complete Secondary School course.

STAGE I. PRELIMINARY

Grammar (see page 4).

If any grammar is done at this stage it will probably be with the intention of helping the Latin work, or the learning of another language. The main points to bring out are:

1. Structure of simple sentence.
2. Meaning of nominative and accusative.
3. Chief parts of speech.
4. Meaning of concord.

(Some of the exercises given in Stage II will be found useful.)

Examples should also be given from other languages learnt by the pupils.

Syllabus

FIRST TERM

I. THE SIMPLE SENTENCE.

The person or thing talked about: SUBJECT	What is said about it: PREDICATE
Types.	
(*a*) The porter	is over there.
(*b*) The porter	collected the tickets.

Exercises.

i. Adding subjects to predicates. E.g. '...took his book away.'

ii. Adding predicates to subjects. E.g. 'The captain....'

iii. Dividing sentences into subject and predicate.

II. Subject words.

> *Nouns:* common and proper; number; gender.
> *Pronouns:* personal; relative.

III. Predicate words.

> *Verbs: action or state.*
>> Types. (*a*) 'He made a boat.'
>>   (*b*) 'He is a boatman.'
>
>> *tense:* past, present, future.

Exercises.

   i. Picking out nouns, and substituting pronouns.

  ii. Substituting nouns for pronouns.

 iii. Picking out verbs and saying whether they are verbs of action or of state.

 iv. Naming and changing tenses in sentences.

SECOND TERM

I. Revision of previous term's work.

II. Limiting or modifying meaning.

> *Adjectives:* quality and quantity.
> *Adverbs:* manner (or quality).

III. Nominative and Accusative: noun forms and personal pronoun forms.

>> Nominative—subject.
>> Accusative—object.
>> *Genitive* (possessive). '*s* and *s*'.

Exercises.

   i. Supplying suitable limitations for subjects and predicates. E.g. 'The...man spoke....'

  ii. Picking out parts of speech.

 iii. Stating cases of nouns and pronouns.

 iv. Making up sentences containing the following adverbs: *correctly, deeply, daily*, etc. Not more than two adverbs may be used in one sentence.

v. Making up a short passage containing these adjectives: *pink, prim, dirty, sulky*.

THIRD TERM

I. REVISION of previous term's work.

II. CONCORD.

> *Adjectives: this* and *that*.
>
> *Pronouns:*
>
> > *personal.* 'His mother gave him a book, which he read to her in the evenings.'
> >
> > *relative.* 'This is the boy who lost his way.' 'This is the boy whom I saw.' 'This is the boy whose hat I found.'

III. ANALYSIS of simple sentences.

> *Exercises.*
>
> i. Supplying missing forms of *this* or *that*. E.g. '...book is not as interesting as...books.'
>
> ii. Supplying correct relative pronouns. E.g. 'This is the man...they robbed.'
>
> iii. Analysis of simple sentences.

IV. REVISION of year's work.

The Writing of English.

During the early Stages it is well to make a broad distinction between the mechanical side of writing and the expression of ideas on paper. At this age the first entails much effort, and often such concentration that it becomes a task to put down things in writing. It is best therefore not to insist on much written composition, but at present to stress the acquirement of facility in the mechanics of the subject, and to give practice in expression orally, with occasional written work where the subject-matter has either been carefully talked over beforehand, or is so well known that there will be the least possible call for puzzling over facts and ideas during the actual writing.

Mechanics of Writing

I. PENMANSHIP.

Script writing has proved a useful beginning in penmanship for young children; its chief disadvantage is that it lacks character. If it is used then a fine pen should be avoided. A more satisfactory cursive hand is taught in Graily Hewitt's *Oxford Copy Books*.

Practice should be for short periods only; ten minutes at a time are sufficient so that attention can be maintained on writing legibly and with some care for arrangement. This last point is of importance from the beginning, so that sound habits of setting out work may be formed as early as possible.

Short fables, one or two verses from poems the pupils choose themselves, and humorous anecdotes are suitable material for this kind of work.

II. SPELLING.

Consonants and vowels; prefix and suffix.

The following rules (taken from R. B. Morgan's *The Groundwork of English*) should be learnt (First term, Rules 1–4; Second term, Rules 5–7).

(1) In words like *mat*, *pet*, *bit*, *mop*, *tub*, the vowel is short. When we add a vowel suffix we must double the final consonant of such words.

Final -*e* makes a syllable long.

(2) Words ending in -*e* drop the -*e* before a vowel suffix, but retain it before a consonant suffix.

(3) In words of more than one syllable, if the final syllable is not accented and ends in a single consonant preceded by a short vowel, the final consonant is not doubled.

(4) Final *l* is always doubled except when it is preceded by a double vowel.

(5) Final *e* after *c* and *g* makes these consonants soft. The *e* is retained before suffixes beginning with *a* and *o* but dropped before suffixes beginning with *e* and *i*.

(6) Words ending in *y* preceded by a consonant change the *y* into *i* when a suffix is added, except when the suffix begins with *i*. Words ending in *y* preceded by a vowel remain unchanged when a suffix is added.

(7) When the vowel sound rhyming with *tea* is produced by the vowels *i* and *e*, *i* always comes before *e* except after *c*, when *e* comes first. (If the vowel sound produced by the two vowels is other than the one rhyming with *tea*, *e* always goes before *i*.)

Practice.

    i. Adding endings to given suffixes. E.g. *sap*, *run*.

    ii. Adding *-able*. E.g. *move*, *blame*.

    iii. Adding prefixes such as *in-*, *re-*.

    iv. Forming words from such given ones as *agree*, *excel*, etc.

    v. Short passages of Dictation; generally these should have been read beforehand.

    vi. Selecting suitable word from several of similar sound, to complete a sentence. E.g. *to*, *too*, *two*.

        (1) —— much pudding is bad for footballers.

        (2) He went —— town.

        (3) —— and —— make four.

III. PUNCTUATION.

Use of Capital Letters

As soon as the idea of a sentence is realised, the use of the *full stop* should be pointed out.

Question mark and *quotation marks* should be studied from the reading book, and sentences dictated without punctuation, or written on the board for the pupils to come out and add punctuation.

The *comma* is a difficulty with young pupils as any rules framed are too technical to be of much use. Observation of the use of commas in books will help. The danger to guard against is the tendency to put in too many commas.

Use of Words

Types of exercise.

   i. Distinguishing between words of similar sound. E.g. *mane, main*; *pair, pear, pare*; *tide, tied*, etc.

     In this type of exercise a sentence should be made up containing the word.

  ii. Completing lists of allied words. E.g. *spring, summer, winter*.

 iii. Completing sentences. E.g. 'Dogs have hair, cats have....'

 iv. Noises. E.g. 'The noise of a whip is called....'

  v. Words for given subjects. E.g. words connected with electric light.

 vi. Difference between *to lie* and *to lay*.

vii. Filling gaps. E.g. 'The...mountain with the...torrent and the...cascades formed a...scene of ...beauty.'

The meanings of new words used in conversation or in reading should be given, and the pupils asked to construct other sentences containing them.

Oral Composition

(*a*) Ten minutes' general questioning and answer should be part of every English period. The subjects might be about the school, the town, places visited, etc. Pupils should also be encouraged to ask questions of the teacher, particularly about things they have not understood in reading, or on placards, etc. This work will need careful preparation by the teacher, so that the questions he asks require more than a word or two in answer. E.g. 'How does a policeman control the traffic?' not, 'What is the name of the church in Broad Street?'

(*b*) Pupils should occasionally describe for the class any outings they have had, such as a picnic, a visit to the Zoo, etc.

(c) Talks about pictures displayed. Posters are particularly useful for this kind of work. The picture should be displayed for a few minutes and the pupils told to ask for any explanations they may need. After the picture has been removed questions should be asked which will call on powers of observation. E.g. the Bovril poster, 'Prevents that sinking feeling', might be used, and the pupils asked for example to describe the man's pyjamas.

(d) During the reading of books there will be many opportunities for oral work. E.g. re-tellings of incidents; descriptions of scenes.

(e) Simple explanations of how to do things. E.g. how to clean teeth, how to treat a cut finger.

(f) Dramatic work also comes under this heading, but will be treated under 'Reading'. (See p. 30.)

(g) Some of the suggestions given below (p. 37) in Stage II can also be used here.

Written Composition

(a) Postcards. Use real ones! The postcard at once limits quantity, and is less alarming than a sheet of blank paper. The pupils should be taught how to write the address. Subjects should appeal to the imagination. E.g. 'You are in Switzerland. Write a postcard home saying that you have had a safe journey. Say something about the journey.'

(b) Some of the answers given to questions on posters, etc., should be written down.

(c) Writing about animals. This always captures interest. E.g. 'Describe how your kitten (puppy) plays.'

(d) Autobiographies. E.g. 'My school cap.'

(e) Subjects such as the following should be set; not more than ten lines should be required at first.

The contents of your pocket.	Fireworks.
	Blind man's buff.
Our road.	What I like to read.
Out of my window.	Getting wet.
A visit to the barber.	How I come to school.

The Reading of English.

Reading aloud by pupils and teacher is an important part of work at this Stage. In addition to the books used in school, other books should be used by the teacher, and the pupils encouraged to bring their own favourites from which to read extracts.

Prose

Aesop, *Fables*.
Padraic Colum, *The Children of Odin*.
James Blaikie, *Wonder Tales of the Ancient World*.
Kipling, *Just-So Stories*.
De la Mare, *Told Again*.
Tales from the *Arabian Nights*.
Thompson Seton's *Animal Stories*.
Dasent, *Tales from the Norse*. (See Nelson's *Fifteen Norse Tales*.)

(For other suitable books, see library lists, pp. 92 and 93.)

Two or three books such as the above should be chosen, and in addition a book of selections such as Wilson's *Pattern Prose* (Nelson).

The method employed should have in view,

1. Increasing the pupils' vocabularies by attention to new words.

2. Giving them the joy of story and myth.

The first of these aims can be best achieved in reading aloud and by getting the pupils to ask for any meaning they do not know. There will always be some words that the teacher will realise are known to a few only in the class; these words he should select beforehand and put on the board; in this way too frequent interruption of the reading will be avoided. The second aim can be best reached by using the play-way; stories should be re-told dramatically by the pupils pretending to be the various people. Improvised properties should be used, and whenever possible the actual re-telling should be done in the school hall or out of doors, so that there may be room for movement. The method is further developed in Stage II. (See p. 40.)

Verse

There are many available collections of miscellaneous verse published for the use of young children; verse specially written for them is seldom helpful. (See p. 92.) No poem should be dwelt upon at any length; by reading aloud the pleasures of rhythm and of sound should be communicated to the pupils. They should be allowed to choose verses for learning; this should be a regular part of the work.

STAGE II. FIRST YEAR OF SCHOOL CERTIFICATE COURSE

Grammar.

The aim at this Stage should be to make clear the nature of a sentence, and the functions of the chief Parts of Speech.

Time. One period a week will probably be required, but explanation by the teacher should not be more than ten minutes in length during any one lesson; this explanation should be followed by oral exercises as varied as possible in nature, with occasional written work.

It may be found better at times not to have a special grammar lesson, but to spread out the work over several lessons, and to give a quarter of an hour to grammar and the remaining time to other English work.

Methods. It is most important in all grammar work to keep the pupils as actively engaged as possible; oral questioning should be the chief means of building up knowledge, varied by blackboard work by the pupils. The 'search' type of question is valuable; the pupils are asked to look for further examples of some particular type of sentence, etc., in the books they read—not only their English books but other text-books they have.

Exercises should be constructive as well as analytical; e.g. in dealing with various kinds of sentences, the pupils should be asked to make up examples of their own.

All grammar work at this stage should be done in school

and not set as homework or preparation; this will mini-
mise the chances of mistakes becoming bad habits.

*Examples should also be given from other languages learnt by
the pupils.*

Syllabus

FIRST TERM

I. THE SIMPLE SENTENCE.

Subject	Predicate
Noun	Verb

Types.

    (*a*) 'Boys speak.'
    (*b*) 'Boys make boxes.'
    (*c*) 'You are boys.'

Exercises.

    i. Making up sentences containing noun as Subject,
      and simple verb as Predicate.
    ii. Making up sentences with noun as Subject, verb,
      and noun as Object.
    iii. Picking out examples of each type.

II. KINDS OF SIMPLE SENTENCE.

    (*a*) Statement. 'Boys wear coats.'
    (*b*) Question. 'Do all boys wear coats?'
    (*c*) Command. 'Put on your coat.'
    (*d*) Wish. 'Good luck to you.'
    (*e*) Exclamation. 'What a hat!'

Exercises.

    i. Framing other examples of these types.
    ii. Picking out other examples.

III. SUBJECT AND PREDICATE.

    (*a*) *Subject:* Nouns—kinds, number. Pronouns—
      kinds, person and number.

Exercises.

   i. Picking out nouns and pronouns stating kinds, number, etc.

   ii. Substituting pronouns for nouns.

     (*b*) *Predicate:* Verbs—finite and infinite; tense—present, past, future; transitive and intransitive.

Objects and Complements.

Exercises.

   i. Picking out verbs stating whether finite or infinite, transitive or intransitive, etc.

   ii. Analysing suitable sentences into Subject (noun or pronoun); Predicate (verb, etc.).

   iii. Constructing sentences to satisfy given analyses; e.g. noun-subject, transitive verb, pronoun-object.

SECOND TERM

I. Revision of previous term's work. This should be thoroughly done, by means of much oral questioning.

II. Subjects and Objects: limitations (enlargements, attributes).

   Type sentences.

     (*a*) 'The boy caught the dog.'

     (*b*) 'The small boy caught the dog.'

     (*c*) 'The small boy caught the black dog.'

Consideration of these leads to function of *adjective*.

Attributive and predicative uses of adjectives.

Kinds and degrees of adjectives.

Exercises.

   i. Making up sentences to satisfy given schemes; e.g. noun-subject with enlargement—Predicate (verb and object).

   ii. Picking out adjectives and saying what kinds they are, and giving other degrees where possible.

III. PREDICATES: limitations (modifications, extensions) of verb.

>   *Types.* (*a*) 'The boy laughed.'
>   (*b*) 'The boy laughed loudly.'

>   Leads to consideration of *adverb*: kinds and degrees.

   Exercises.

   i. Picking out adverbs and state kinds.
   ii. Modifying verbs in given sentences by adverbs.

THIRD TERM

I.   REVISION of previous work.

II. CONCORDS. See above, p. 25.

III. PREPOSITIONS. It is important by means of examples to make clear the difference in function between adverb and preposition. A large number of examples should be then chosen by the pupils from their books, and sentences constructed in which the same word is used (*a*) as adverb, (*b*) as preposition, (*c*) as conjunction.

IV. INTERJECTIONS AND CONJUNCTIONS.

V.   REVISION EXERCISES.

>   *Types.*

>   i. Analysing of simple sentences.
>   ii. Picking out various parts of speech and saying all that is known of them.
>   iii. Constructing sentences to given schemes.
>   iv. Outline parsing of words in suitable sentences.

The Writing of English.

The work at this Stage should still be mainly of an oral nature, though more written work may be expected than in the previous years. It will be found necessary to vary the work in any one period; not, for instance, to give the whole time to grammar, but to spend ten minutes on that subject, twenty minutes on oral work such as reading, and so on.

Mechanics of Writing

I. PENMANSHIP.

Copybook work is of doubtful value as the pupil is either faced with an almost impossible standard of excellence, or has to imitate the work of metal engravers. Mrs Bridges' *New Handwriting Cards* (Oxford University Press) have proved useful as setting a normal standard of achievement in legibility. Such cards should be used as standards and not as models.

To give purpose and interest to handwriting the keeping of a commonplace book is strongly recommended. In this the pupil copies out any verses, or passages of prose that he likes; the aim should be to set out each extract in pleasing writing and with regard to page proportion.

A more formal hand should be taught in the Art classes, for such purposes as Notices, Christmas Cards, etc.

Throughout the schoolwork, in all subjects, insistence on legibility and good setting-out will do much to cultivate sound habits in handwriting.

II. SPELLING.

The following aids to spelling should be used at this stage:

(1) A note-book—alphabetical—should be kept for entering,

     (*a*) words mis-spelt in writing; these are entered *correctly* spelt,

     (*b*) new words from reading or speaking; meanings should also be entered with a sentence including the word,

     (*c*) a few guidance rules; e.g. use of EI and IE,

     (*d*) short lists of common words ending in -ANCE, -ENCE, -ABLE, -IBLE,

     (*e*) groups of words having similar sounds but different spellings and meanings.

(2) Dictation of passages previously read and explained; the dictation should come some days after the reading.

III. PUNCTUATION.

The use of the full-stop, comma, question and quotation marks should be studied from books used for reading.

Exercises.

   i. Dictation of short sentences without stating punctuation.

   ii. Paragraphs without full-stops.

   iii. Conversations to be written down with correct punctuation; these should be very brief, and arise out of class conversation.

Use of Words

Exercises such as the following will often be occasioned by reading, and it is better that they should arise naturally in that way than always be set separately.

   i. Make a list of words connected with *fire*.

   ii. Give words opposite in meaning to *back*, *push*, etc.

   iii. Give words similar in meaning to *fault*, *weak*, etc.

   iv. Make up a sentence containing these words, in any order, *plumber*, *bathroom*, *burst*, *tools*, *mate*.

   v. Look up in the dictionary the meanings of these words, *intelligent*, *cross* (noun), *novelty*, *reliance*, etc.

   vi. Give a single word for the following, *to go different ways*.

   vii. Make lists of nouns, verbs and adjectives connected with the word *black*.

Oral Composition

(*a*) Questions on books read. It has long been a custom to insist on what have been called 'full answers', or 'complete sentences'. Where a single word gives the right answer, it is silly to ask for 'a complete sentence'. Such unnatural requirements divorce schoolwork from ordinary life. Questions should be so framed that generally a number of words will be required to give a satisfactory, i.e. intelligent, answer. E.g. to ask, 'Did Robinson Crusoe see a footprint on the sand?' is rightly answered by 'Yes'; to insist on 'Robinson Crusoe did see a footprint on the sand' serves no useful purpose. The question might have been framed, 'What did Robinson do when he saw the footprint on the sand?' This will require (*a*) recollection of more than a single fact, (*b*) an attempt to get events in their right order, and (*c*) the clear expression of facts—in other words, the exercise of those things on which all good composition depends.

(*b*) Short verbal descriptions of THINGS SEEN; e.g. a football match related by several pupils in turn; a street incident; what I see on my way to school, etc.

(*c*) Similar descriptions of PLACES VISITED; and of PEOPLE MET.

(*d*) Accounts of stories read out of school.

(*e*) Descriptions of HOW TO DO, HOW TO MAKE, HOW TO PLAY. E.g. how to wrap up and fasten a parcel; how to lay a fire; how to make a paper hat; how to fly a kite; how to sharpen a pencil.

(*f*) Descriptions of posters, and of pictures seen in books, or displayed for a short time.

(*g*) Simple dramatisation of stories read in class; these should be chiefly dialogues at first. Ballads should also be used for this purpose. (See READING OF ENGLISH below.)

Written Composition

(*a*) Occasionally some of the answers given in oral work should be written down afterwards.

(*b*) Completion of fables and short stories. E.g. Complete the following story in ten lines of writing.

A good man had several quarrelsome sons. He decided to teach them a lesson, so he made a birch of many twigs, and calling them together he said, 'Try each of you to break that birch'. They tried with all the power they had, but failed to break the birch. Then the father said, 'Untie the bundle of twigs, and try to break each separately'....

(*c*) Composite stories on pictures. The whole class discusses a suitable picture, such as one of the historical frescoes in the Houses of Parliament. They decide on a story that would fit the picture. The writing out of such a story would be too long a task for pupils of this age, so each is given a short portion to write out. These parts are then collected and read aloud in sequence, the pupils suggesting improvements for filling gaps, etc.

(*d*) Imaginary island stories should be written in similar fashion; the first island should be drawn on the board by one pupil and improvements and suitable names suggested by the others.

(*e*) Outlines to be filled. E.g.

Thirsty crow—large jar of water—could not reach water—tries pushing jar over—too heavy—tries breaking—too strong—drops pebbles in—water rises till high enough.

(*f*) Telegrams. Can be made more interesting if real forms are used, and pupils send messages and replies to each other.

(*g*) Letters. A certain amount of instruction must first be given in letter forms, addressing envelopes, etc. This should be as real as possible; letter paper and envelopes should always be used. The pupils should write letters to each other.

(*h*) Single paragraphs describing objects without naming them; success is proved by other pupils naming objects after the descriptions have been read aloud; e.g.

It is about one inch high, made of white porcelain, the bottom is a smaller circle than the top—Inkwell.

The Reading of English.

READING ALOUD. This should be a definite and important part of the work at this stage, but care must be taken that the reading does not become lifeless; the reading of any text by turns round the class is apt to become meaningless for most of the pupils once they have taken part.

Reading aloud by the teacher should set a standard of excellence and of interest. He will occasionally read aloud passages from the class books, but he should also devote a whole period four or five times a term to the reading aloud of short stories, descriptive passages, etc., that will help to capture the pupils' interest in new authors, or in new types of literature.

The pupils should be encouraged to bring along books they have enjoyed reading at home, and to read aloud parts they particularly like; if they know that there will be periods set aside for this purpose, they will be on the look-out for suitable material.

Prose

Renderings of old legends, myths, etc., will be found useful at this stage. The following amongst others may be suggested:

Hawthorne, *Tanglewood Tales*, and *Wonder Book*.
Kingsley, *Heroes*, and *Water Babies*.
Tales from the *Iliad*, and *Odyssey*.
Tales from the Icelandic Sagas.
Don Quixote.
Defoe, *Robinson Crusoe*.
Swift, *Gulliver's Travels*.
Hull, *Cuchulain*.
Rolleston, *The High Deeds of Finn*.
The Mabinogion.
Stories of King Arthur and his Knights.

(For other suitable books, see library lists, pp. 92 and 93.)

Stories from the Bible should be read occasionally, preferably in an edition printed in the normal fashion of other books.

Method. The play-method is most effective at this age. A story is first read aloud by the teacher; if possible it should then be read by the pupils representing characters, and one pupil reading the descriptive and connecting narrative. The class is then divided into groups, and each group is given a portion of the story to dramatise in a simple fashion; the aim is not so much to produce a play, as to provide real opportunities for each pupil to speak and act a part. When the whole has been roughed out in this fashion, the various parts are put together, and the dramatic version acted by groups of the class according to the number of characters required. As much reality as possible should be given to the work by using improvised properties, and costumes. A story-teller may be needed to give continuity to the various scenes. It is most important to see that each pupil, whatever his abilities, should have an opportunity of taking an important part in the representation; the temptation is to give to the naturally gifted pupils the major parts. They need the practice less than the others.

Example of treatment. The following division into scenes was made by a class of boys who were reading Kingsley's 'Perseus', from *The Heroes.*

   I. *Story-teller*; the birth and early life of Perseus.

   II. Perseus and Pallas Athené.

   III. Perseus and Polydectes; the present and the boast.

   IV. Perseus and Pallas Athené and Hermes.

   V. The journey to the Gorgon.

      i. The three grey sisters.

      ii. The nymphs.

   VI. The slaying of the Gorgon.

   VII. Perseus and Andromeda; the rescue.

   VIII. The return; and the death of Polydectes.

   IX. Perseus and Acrisius.

The class was divided into groups, and scenes allotted to each; the scenes were acted first in front of all the boys, and criticisms asked for. This was followed by a revision of the whole, and a Grand Performance of the complete series. A story-teller linked up the various scenes by describing what had happened during the intervals.

This occupied a term, with an average of an hour a week devoted to the work.

Explanation of new words, etc., will naturally arise in the course of the reading and dramatisation. In using such stories as *The Heroes* great care should be taken to get the correct pronunciation of the proper names.

Verse

An anthology of story and ballad poems will be found most suitable at this Stage. The collection should be as varied and as large as possible, as no one poem should be laboured, or minutely dissected.

The teacher should read aloud the poems and then get the pupils to read any verses they particularly like; in this way the effectiveness of the pictures called up in the imagination will be made apparent and the music of the verse be allowed to make its appeal. A few questions should be asked, and occasionally some written work set in re-telling an incident.

After the first term, it should be possible for the pupils to make up ballad poems of their own, either collectively or separately.

Typical questions.

(*a*) What do you think is the story behind this ballad?

(*b*) Which verse calls up the most vivid picture?

(*c*) Write an additional verse giving more details of....

(*d*) Describe one of the people in the ballad.

(*e*) Pick out the line you like most.

(*f*) Re-tell the story as *X* might have told it.

Repetition. The pupils should be allowed to choose the poems they would like to learn for themselves; whatever has been learned should be spoken in front of the others.

'Elocution', as popularly understood, must be avoided; attention should be concentrated on clear enunciation, and the right expression of the music of the verse.

STAGE III. SECOND YEAR

Grammar.

The aim during this year is to reach an understanding of the meaning of phrase, sentence, clause, and of the *functions* of the different kinds of subordinate clauses.

Time. One hour a week of concentrated work will be needed. If this is done during this year, much time and labour will be saved in future years.

Method. Much oral work in searching for examples and answering questions about them will prove profitable. More paper work can be done than in the previous year, and an occasional homework exercise, when the main principles have been thoroughly understood.

Examples should also be given from other languages learnt by the pupils.

Syllabus

FIRST TERM

I. REVISION of previous term's work. Several periods should be devoted to this—oral work—to make quite sure that the groundwork of the previous year has been well laid.

II. MEANING of *phrase and sentence.*

    Types. (*a*) 'An energetic boy.'
          (*b*) 'This boy is energetic.'

Exercises.

  i. Picking out phrases.

  ii. Substituting phrases for adjectives and adverbs.

  iii. Making up different kinds of phrases.

  iv. Turning phrases into sentences, and *vice versa.*

SECOND TERM

I. SENTENCES AND CLAUSES.

Multiple (compound, composite); complex.

(a) Principal (main) clause.

(b) Subordinate clauses.

Types.

(a) Multiple: 'He set the candle down on the
table, and then drew the curtains and put a
fresh log on the fire'.

(b) Complex: 'He set the candle down on the
table which stood in front of the fire'.

II. KINDS OF SUBORDINATE CLAUSES.

(i) Adjective Clauses

Types.

(a) 'The boat that was lying on the beach belonged
to an old fisherman.'

(b) 'The man who stopped us wore a light brown
coat.'

(c) 'The town where we spent our holidays was
full of visitors.'

(d) 'The speaker whom you heard at the dinner,
was the President.'

Exercises.

i. Picking out adjective clauses.

ii. Substituting clauses for adjectives.

iii. Analysing sentences into clauses.

III. THE RELATIVE PRONOUN. Case.

Exercise. Picking out and parsing relative pronouns.

THIRD TERM

I. REVISION of previous term's work.

II. KINDS OF SUBORDINATE CLAUSES.

(ii) Adverb Clauses

Types.

(a) Time. 'I will come when you send word.'

(b) Place. 'He put the letter where she could find it.'

(c) Purpose. 'They buried the treasure so that no one would find it without a clue.'

(d) Condition. 'The fire-engine will come if you ring the alarum.'

(e) Reason or Cause. 'He could not come because he had a cold.'

(f) Consequence. 'They worked so hard that they finished early.'

(g) Concession. 'Although the weather was bad, they set sail.'

(h) Comparison. 'He walked faster than his brother (walked).'

(i) Manner. 'The Chairman spoke as few Chairmen can speak.'

(j) Degree. 'He ran as hard as he could.'

Exercises.

i. Picking out adverb clauses.

ii. Making up different kinds of adverb clauses.

iii. Substituting clauses for words.

iv. Analysing into clauses. Examples should be chosen containing both adjective and adverb clauses.

v. Constructing sentences to satisfy given schemes; e.g. principal clause—adverb clause of reason.

NOTE. The list of types of adverb clauses should not be given to be learnt by rote, but be kept in the English note-book for reference purposes.

The Writing of English.

Mechanics of Writing

I. PENMANSHIP.

The commonplace book should still be used for copying out any verses or passages of prose that appeal to the pupils.

Legibility should be the first consideration in all written work; good setting-out is also important.

II. SPELLING.

The note-book to contain lists of words mis-spelt should be continued, and from time to time looked over to see if the same words have been recorded frequently. Against each word entered the dictionary definition should be written, and an illustrative sentence added.

III. PUNCTUATION.

Ambiguity due to wrong punctuation should be freely illustrated by sentences taken, for example, from *Punch*, and from the pupils' own work. Passages of prose should be occasionally studied for the punctuation alone. Dictation without indication of punctuation is a useful exercise.

Use of Words

Lessons should be given on

    i. the use of the dictionary—not for etymological purposes,

    ii. prefixes and suffixes,

    iii. importance of order.

Illustrations of these topics should be taken from books read in school, and the pupils should be asked to search for additional examples.

Exercises.

    i. Common synonyms to use in sentences in such a way that the differences in meaning and use are brought out clearly.

    ii. Single words for definitions; e.g. put right again, unable to speak.

    iii. Supplying appropriate adjectives, etc. E.g. I prefer an...to a sedentary life.

    iv. Forming words from other parts of speech; e.g. give nouns and adjectives corresponding to the following verbs: *observe, prove, denounce.*

    v. Giving antonyms and homonyms.

    vi. Defining words.

    vii. Grouping words according to subjects; e.g. classify the words that follow under the headings (1) health, (2) prosperity—*success, vigour, hale, affluence, lucky, robust, flourish, hearty.*

Oral Composition

(a) Descriptions of things done; e.g. experiments in science work, how to make models, how to do common jobs such as fire-lighting, etc.

(b) Ten-minute lectures on hobbies.

(c) Answers to questions on books read.

(d) Re-telling of stories read to class, or read out of class.

(e) Accounts of local events; e.g. opening of new buildings, etc.

(f) Reports of school affairs; e.g. matches.

(g) Descriptions of walks in the neighbourhood, visits to places of interest, etc.

(h) Descriptions of objects seen; e.g. in a museum.

(i) Descriptions of pictures shown to the class for a short time.

NOTE.. In all exercises such as the above, great stress should be laid on accuracy of observation, as without this no good writing is possible.

Written Composition

(a) Letters of all kinds; e.g. to friends, to other pupils, to imaginary characters, to characters from fiction, to shopkeepers, etc.

(b) Paragraphs of local news as if for a newspaper, or for a class magazine.

(c) Short compositions on subjects familiar to pupils.

(*d*) Written work based on previous oral composition as suggested above.

(*e*) Descriptions of characters in books read.

(*f*) Expansion of incidents from novels and plays.

(*g*) Accounts of visits paid to places.

(*h*) Completion of partly related stories.

(*i*) Short outlines of plots of novels read, or of films seen.

(*j*) Imaginary diaries, logs, autobiographies.

(*k*) Writing advertisements.

(*l*) Descriptions of other pupils.

(*m*) Summaries of important paragraphs in school textbooks.

(*n*) Notes for ten-minute lectures.

(*o*) Reports of ten-minute lectures.

(*p*) Dialogues between imaginary, or historical characters.

(*q*) Accounts of scenes from history.

(*r*) Stories suggested by pictures.

(*s*) Stories based on treasure-island maps.

The Reading of English.

READING ALOUD. The teacher should read aloud frequently from books that he thinks will capture the interest of the pupils. These might well be by modern writers such as W. H. Hudson, Kipling, R. L. Stevenson, Buchan, Quiller-Couch, Kenneth Grahame, De la Mare, James Stephens, etc. Varied selections from such authors are a great aid to developing taste in good literature. The readings should not be restricted to prose, but should include selections from poets of all periods.

The pupils themselves should also be encouraged to read aloud passages, etc., they themselves have chosen from their own reading.

Prose

The following is a selection of useful books for careful reading.

Cambridge Readings in Literature (or similar book of prose extracts)

and two of the following:

Dickens, *Christmas Stories*.
Irving, *Rip Van Winkle*, etc.
Kingsley, *Westward Ho!* and *Hereward the Wake*.
Scott, *Tales of a Grandfather*.
Lamb, *Tales from Shakespeare*.
Re-tellings of Froissart's *Chronicles* and of Chaucer's *Canterbury Tales*.
Stephens, *Irish Fairy Tales*.
Animal stories by Thompson Seton, Roberts, etc.

(For other suitable books, see library lists, pp. 94 and 95.)

The book of prose extracts will be in use throughout the year. No attempt should be made to read the other two books entirely aloud during a term, but the bulk of the reading should be done silently in class, and at home. The pupils should then be asked to bring up any difficulties they have met—apart from meanings which they should look up for themselves in their dictionaries. During these readings the pupils should look up in their dictionaries any words they do not understand, and make a note of them in their note-books. Any other difficulties they meet should be raised during a period set aside for that purpose. The teacher may find it useful to introduce a book, or even to give a brief outline of its contents, provided he doesn't rob the pupils of the pleasures of anticipation. After this first fairly rapid reading, the pupils should be asked to select the most striking scenes; these should then be dramatised after the fashion set out in the first year syllabus (see p. 40). A higher standard of result should now be expected than in the previous year; more attention will be given to getting a connected presentation, and to interpreting the characters.

At the end of each term, the play should be written out in a class commonplace book, each player writing out some of his own part.

The use of books as the basis for written composition has been already mentioned.

Verse

The books should include

An anthology suitable for pupils of 12 to 13 years.
One or two longer poems, such as

Longfellow, *Hiawatha*.
Macaulay, *Lays of Ancient Rome*.
Matthew Arnold, *Sohrab and Rustum*, and *Balder Dead*.

Or, a collection of a few longer narrative poems.

All poems should be read aloud by the teacher, or, in part, by the pupils.

Quantity and variety are desirable at this stage; no poem should be laboured, or used for other purposes than bringing the pleasure of poetry to the pupils.

Opportunities may arise when the subject of metre will call for comment, but not for detailed treatment.

Verse writing should be encouraged, not as an exercise, but for interest; all pupils should not be expected to write verse, but the success of one will soon encourage others to test their powers, and to find out if this is a medium of expression for them.

The learning of whole poems, or of chosen verses, should form part of the work; the speaking of verse before the class is important; the pupils are more likely to be successful in this work if they are generally allowed to choose poems or verses that appeal to them.

STAGE IV. THIRD YEAR

Grammar.

The main grammar work should be finished during this year. If the three years' course has been thoroughly done, the pupils should have a sufficient knowledge to apply to the other languages they may learn, and to understand the nature of faults in their own writing.

Examples should also be given from other languages learnt by the pupils.

Syllabus

FIRST TERM

I. REVISION of previous work. This should be done very thoroughly, special attention being given to the complex sentence and adjective and adverb clauses.

II. KINDS OF SUBORDINATE CLAUSES.

(iii) Noun Clauses

Types.

(*a*) As subject. 'That you are ill is very clear.'

(*b*) As object. 'We knew that a storm was coming.'

(*c*) As complement. 'This seems what he wanted.'

(*d*) In apposition. 'The fact that he was too lazy was obvious.'

(*e*) After a preposition. 'They asked the shopmen for what they required.'

Exercises.

i. Picking out and naming noun clauses.

ii. Making up noun clauses of the various types.

iii. Making up sentences to satisfy given schemes, e.g. principal clause—noun clause (object).

SECOND TERM

I. DIRECT AND INDIRECT (REPORTED) SPEECH.

Exercises.

   i. Re-writing passages from books read, and from newspapers into either form.

   ii. Writing reports of what has been said in class.

   iii. Putting reported lectures, etc., into direct form.

II. ANALYSIS of complex sentences into clauses.

This will occupy a greater part of the term's work in grammar. Much should be done orally until it is clear that all the pupils understand the nature of the clauses. Discussion of long sentences is valuable; examples should be drawn not only from books read in class, but also from the pupils' own writings.

THIRD TERM

I. THE VERB INFINITIVE.

   (*a*) Infinitive mood as noun. E.g. 'To read improves the mind'.

   (*b*) Gerund (Verb-noun). E.g. 'Studying Latin improves the mind'.

   (*c*) Participle (Verb-adjective, Gerundive). E.g. 'I saw the boy reading his book'.

II. WORDS AS DIFFERENT PARTS OF SPEECH.

Examples.

   i. Sir Launcelot was a *Knight* of the Round Table. (Noun.)
      King Arthur *knighted* the squire. (Verb.)

   ii. Red as a *rose* is she. (Noun.)
      A *rose* window is sometimes called a wheel window. (Adjective.)

   iii. Keep *what* I tell you secret. (Pronoun.)
      What street does he live in? (Adjective.)

The teacher should collect a number of examples of this kind, as the consideration of them helps to emphasise the functions of words.

III. Parsing.

Exercises in parsing are valuable where the pupils are learning other languages. An occasional exercise should be set, with particular emphasis on verbs.

IV. Revision.

The Writing of English.

The work of the previous years should have laid the foundation for more advanced written composition in the third and following years. Up to this stage the aim has been to get clear expression of familiar ideas and knowledge. Greater emphasis should now be put upon arrangement and sequence. So far not more than three or four paragraphs have been the extent of the written work; from now onwards a series of connected paragraphs carefully thought out as a whole should be expected.

Mechanics of Writing

I. Penmanship.

Apart from insisting on legibility, little should need to be done on this topic. The commonplace book will still be in use.

II. Spelling and Punctuation.

The spelling note-book should be kept up to date, and periodically revised. Exercises in punctuation should take the form of

    i. occasional dictation,

    ii. unpunctuated passages to re-write,

    ii. passages of older English to modernise,

    iv. discussion of an occasional passage from the point of view of its punctuation.

Use of Words

Considerable practice should be given in the use of words in order to extend the vocabulary. The dictionary should always be at hand, not only in the English lessons, but at all times. Pupils should make lists of all words they look up, and add the dictionary definition, with connected words, and sentences to illustrate the use. Early in the first term of the year, a lesson should be devoted to the use of the dictionary, not only for the meanings of English words, but for work in other languages.

Exercises.

i. Supplying for given words, where possible, synonyms, antonyms.

ii. Writing sentences to bring out the meanings of synonyms.

iii. Supplying lists of nouns, adjectives, verbs, adverbs, etc., for a given subject; e.g. speech. (*Nouns:* talk, oration, etc., *adjectives:* oral, eloquent, etc., *verbs:* recite, utter, etc., *adverbs:* orally, etc.)

iv. Grading adjectives, etc., according to intensity of meaning; e.g. *pretty, plain, exquisite, beautiful, well-favoured.*

v. Supplying words to fill blanks in given passages. E.g. 'I blanked not a single blank, not so much as a dog to blank me with his blank'.

vi. Picking out the most suitable word from several suggested; e.g. (*amuse, enliven*). He —— the proceedings and —— us with several good stories.

vii. Variation in use of words with different prepositions; e.g. look *at, through, over.*

viii. Meanings of suffixes and prefixes.

Composition

The stage has now been reached when attention can be concentrated on the written composition. Oral work will still be done, but rather incidentally than of set purpose. A wider range of topics will be desirable than in previous years.

I. NOTE-MAKING.

Definite instruction should now be given in how to make and use notes. Passages from school text-books should be used for this purpose. Emphasis must be put upon the value of main headings, sub-headings, etc., and other methods by which the sequence of ideas or events can be kept clear. Occasionally notes of a lesson given in class, or of a lecture, should be asked for. Practice should also be given in writing up from notes taken some time previously.

II. PARAPHRASE.

A beginning should be made in this subject. Exercises for this year should be confined to passages of prose that have presented difficulties in reading, paragraphs of older English; e.g. Clarendon, and troublesome speeches from plays. Poems should not be used for this purpose.

III. COMPOSITION.

Lessons should be given on the following matters with illustrations drawn from books read in class,

   i. collecting ideas,
   ii. arranging ideas,
   iii. planning the composition as a whole; considera-
        tion of proportion.

Types of Subjects.

   i. Familiar topics, such as
      (*a*) descriptions of places, people and things,
      (*b*) accounts of events witnessed,
      (*c*) how to make, and do.

   ii. Accounts of plays, and of books read.

  iii. Composite stories—begun by one pupil and passed
       round for additions.

   iv. Scenes from history in dramatic form.

    v. Short biographies.

   vi. Forecasts of the future.

  vii. Contrasts with the past.

 viii. Diaries, personal or imaginary.

   ix. Articles for the class or school magazine.

    x. Imaginary travels and adventures.

   xi. Inventions and discoveries.

  xii. Answers to questions on books read.

 xiii. Many of the subjects suggested for the second year
       (see pp. 46 and 47) can be treated in a fuller manner.

 xiv. Letters of all kinds.

The Reading of English.

A few lessons should be devoted to reading aloud from modern and other authors; selections should cover as wide a range of interests as possible.

Drama

The practice in the previous years in the making of simple scenes based on books read, or on history, should have laid a good foundation for the reading of plays.

Three plays, one for each term, should be chosen. Two of these might be by Shakespeare, and a third by another dramatist, or several modern one-act plays might be read instead of one long play.

The following will be found suitable:

SHAKESPEARE.
Midsummer Night's Dream; Richard II; Merchant of Venice; As You Like It; Henry V; Julius Caesar.

OTHER DRAMATISTS.
Dekker, *Shoemaker's Holiday;* Sheridan, *Rivals.*

MODERN ONE-ACT PLAYS.

McKinnel, *The Bishop's Candlesticks;* Brighouse, *How the Weather is Made;* Ferguson, *Campbell of Kilmour;* Drinkwater, *Robin Hood and the Pedlar;* Malleson, *Paddly Pools.*

During this year plays should be used mainly for acting purposes. The play chosen should first be read aloud by the teacher without interruption of any kind. In using Shakespeare's plays it will be necessary to shorten and arrange the scenes so that it will be possible to act the version during the term. This work may be done previously by the teacher, or one of the available acting editions adopted for the class, such as *First Steps in Shakespeare* (Cambridge). The method of dividing the class into groups according to the number of characters required, will be found most productive, as in this way each member gets a fair share of the work. If possible a full performance, with improvised properties, should be given before an audience drawn from other pupils in the school.

Example of Treatment.

Richard II

If ten periods are available during the term they could be used as follows:

1–3. Reading aloud by teacher, followed by same portions set as home-reading.

4–6. Reading aloud by pupils taking parts; done in front of the class with some action.

7. Arrangement of class into three groups for preparing acting version and allocating parts.

8–10. Acting version; rehearsed, etc. Followed by special occasion for full performance before school audience.

Acting version: the figures in brackets indicate lines that could be omitted to save time (references to Globe edition).

Act i.	Scene i	(1–83)	} Prepared by Group I.
	Scene iii	(1–98, 249 to end)	
Act ii.	Scene i	(224 to end)	

	Scene iii	(1–67)	} Prepared by Group II.
Act iii.	Scene ii		
	Scene iii	(1–61)	

Act iv.	Scene i	(1–106)	} Prepared by Group III.
Act v.	Scene v	(1–67)	
	Scene vi		

NOTE. In the final performance each group acts its own section: this means three different boys act the part of Richard II, etc. The disadvantages of this are outweighed by the gain in time and increased number of boys taking important characters.

Prose

Two or three books should be chosen for careful reading according to the time available. No book should be used for more than one term. A book of prose extracts for use throughout the school year should also be chosen. Long selections are preferable to short passages.

Suitable Books:

Addison and Steele, Selections from the *Spectator*.
Borrow, *Lavengro*.
Defoe, *Journal of the Plague Year*.
Irving, *Sketch Book*.
Scott, *Ivanhoe*, and *Kenilworth*.
Malory, Selections from *Morte d'Arthur*.
Goldsmith, *Vicar of Wakefield*.
Eliot, *Silas Marner*.
Dickens, *Tale of Two Cities*.
Froude, *English Seamen*.
Reade, *Cloister and the Hearth*.
Blackmore, *Lorna Doone*.
Thackeray, *Henry Esmond*.
A book of Letters.
Stevenson, *Travels with a Donkey*.

A book of Short Stories.
Southey, *Life of Nelson*.
(For other suitable books, see library lists, pp. 95–98.)

The bulk of the reading should be done silently in class,
or as home-reading; occasional passages that have im-
pressed the pupils might be read aloud by them. Words
that they have had to look up in a dictionary should be
entered in their note-books, with the definition and reference to the page where the word came. The teacher
should occasionally look through these note-books chiefly
for the purpose of ascertaining the scope of the pupils'
vocabularies.

It may be helpful with some books to give short talks
on the matter of which they treat; two or three periods
should be spent in talking over with the class what they
have read, and an occasional written composition set,
preferably of an imaginative character.

In addition to the set books, attention should now be
given to the Bible; two lessons in the term might very well
be devoted to reading aloud stories from both Testaments,
and fine passages from them and from the Apocrypha.
Reading-homework should also be set from the Bible.

Example of Treatment.

Froude, *English Seamen*

The teacher should first of all become familiar with the
general history of exploration during this period by reading such books as E. F. Benson's *Drake*, Sir Walter
Raleigh's *Early English Voyages*, and Beazley's *Voyages and
Travels*. The one-volume selection of Hakluyt's *Voyages*,
edited by Payne and Beazley, will provide interesting eye-
witness accounts of some of the incidents described by
Froude. Extracts from these should be read aloud to the
class. For the Armada, Hale's *The Great Armada* should
be consulted.

Several of the volumes in The Golden Hind Series
(Bodley Head) will interest the pupils, such as those on
Raleigh, Hawkins and Frobisher. These should be in-

cluded in the class or school library. The British Museum publishes two contemporary maps of Drake's voyage.

The teacher might introduce the book by giving a general idea of the period of exploration. The first reading should be a silent one, partly done in class and partly at home. Lectures I and v could be omitted during the first reading. A second reading should follow, preceded by the teacher pointing out the main matters of interest and possibly amplifying some incidents by reading extracts from the original accounts given in Hakluyt. It is as well to give a definite purpose to this second reading by suggesting questions for the answering of which the pupils have to gather material as they progress. Such questions as the following would be suitable:

   i. What aspects of his subject seem to have appealed to Froude most strongly?

  ii. How far does the author show his religious bias?

 iii. What impression does he give you of Elizabeth?

 iv. Give references to places where he shows his knowledge of practical seamanship.

  v. Pick out passages which seem particularly successful to you as (*a*) descriptions of action; (*b*) descriptions of people. An opportunity will be given for reading these aloud to the class.

Such questions give a definite object to the reading and help to concentrate attention. When the second reading has been done, then the book could be used as the basis for interesting composition work. Such subjects as the following might be set:

   i. Imagine yourself to be a seaman on *The Golden Hind*; give a few extracts from your diary of the voyage round the world.

  ii. Write a letter from Drake to Hawkins explaining his sailing away from San Juan.

 iii. Report the trial of Mr Doughty.

 iv. Describe the meeting between Drake and Winter after the circumnavigation.

If such a subject as 'The Armada' is set, the result will only be a re-hash of Lectures VIII and IX.

A more ambitious scheme would be the writing of a play about Drake; this will call for a great deal of selective ability and also knowledge on the part of the pupil, far more than is required in the writing of a short biography of Drake.

One formal exercise is worth doing towards the end of the term. Lecture I should be studied as a good example of paragraphing; this will be brought out by making lists of paragraph headings, or by using the Lecture for note-making practice.

The Use of Books.

A certain amount of instruction in the use of books of reference should now be given. Several copies of *Whitaker's Almanack*, and of Smith's *Smaller Classical Dictionary* (Everyman's Library) should be available, and their use explained. Pupils should be encouraged to look up in these information that will help them to overcome difficulties they meet in their reading; for instance, it is far better for them to look up classical references for themselves than for the teacher to give them.

Verse

During this and the succeeding year *The Golden Treasury* will provide the best anthology of English verse. The pupils will be introduced to much of the finest poetry in the language, and care must be taken to avoid dulling their appreciation by ill-advised explanation and over-analysis of content or method. The appeal should be through the ear at first, so much reading aloud by the teacher will produce the best results.

The following scheme is suggested for a series of thirty periods; the object in view has been to give an idea of the variety of English poetry so that each pupil should find something to his taste. During each lesson the teacher should indicate other poems of similar nature for silent reading; he should also supplement the poems from other sources.

The reference numbers are to the latest copyright edition with the additional Fifth Book edited by Laurence Binyon.

1. Songs. 1, 2, 3, 10, 37, 56, 73, 75, 101, 102, 116, 117.
   These are for pure delight and no attempt should yet be made to study these intensively.

2. A lesson on rhythm.
   Examples can be drawn from poems read in the previous lesson.

3. Life and Death. 9, 64, 65, 77, 79, 90, 91, 92, 95, 96.

4. Speaking of verse learnt; or reading aloud by pupils of poems they like.

5. Poems of Andrew Marvell. 88, 105, 141, 142, 146.
   After the reading of the *Horatian Ode*, Lionel Johnson's *By the Statue of King Charles* (413) should be read.

6. A lesson on rhyme.

7. Speaking of verse, etc.

8. *L'Allegro* (144).

9. *Il Penseroso* (145).
   The briefest of notes on the classical allusions should be made, and attention given chiefly to the pictures and the rhyme. Palgrave's own notes are sufficient.

10. Speaking of verse, etc.

11. Romance. 135, 225, 237, 360.
   Previous reading of ballads will supply interesting material for comparisons, etc.

12. Gray's *Elegy* (187).

13. Speaking of verse, etc.

14. Poems of Burns. 161, 176, 184, 190, 191, 196, 197.
   Tam O'Shanter might be read aloud, but it will be necessary to put a list of difficult words on the blackboard first.

15. Verse patterns.
     Examples: 97, 157, 164, 203, 260.
16. Poems of Scott. 213, 227, 240 (read also 241), 248, 278, 281, 285.
17. Speaking of verse, etc.
18. The sonnet. 40, 46, 313.
19. More sonnets. 87, 93, 210, 291, 293.
20. Speaking of verse, etc.
21. Nature: birds. 286, 288, 289, 363, 438.
22. Nature: flowers and trees. 139, 140, 295, 301, 302, 348, 393.
     There must be no forcing of these poems; the pupils will be interested more from the point of view of accuracy of observation at first than from appreciation of nature.
23. Speaking of verse, etc.
24. Nature: the seasons. 345, 349, 350, 351, 365.
25. Sound and sense.
     Poems 85, 340 and 396 will provide examples.
26. Naval poems. 250, 251, 405, 406, 407.
27. Speaking of verse, etc.
28. Ships and the sea. 362, 386, 400, 401, 405.
29. Out of doors. 398, 399, 403, 404, 417.
30. Recital of verse from year's reading and learning.

Pupils should be encouraged from time to time to write verse of their own; successful efforts should be read aloud to the class, and also included in the class magazine, and the best in the school magazine.

Repetition. The following poems from *The Golden Treasury* should be learnt: 87, 92, 184, 210, 237, 291, 349, 362. Parts of 144, 145 and 187 should also be learnt. All other repetition should be of verses chosen by the pupils.

STAGE V. FOURTH YEAR

Grammar

The work during the previous three years should have laid a sound foundation, and there is little need for instruction in formal grammar. The following matters should be included in the year's work:

I. Occasional revision of previous work by means of oral questioning as difficulties are met in reading or writing. Great care, however, should be used in the choice of material on which such questions are based. Fine passages of prose should never be so used; pedestrian prose and the pupils' own compositions supply all that is required. Discussion of the grammatical difficulties of passages for translation into other languages should be arranged between the teachers concerned; a useful exercise is for a piece of translation into English to be discussed not only in the language class from the point of view of accuracy, but in the English class from that of good, clear language.

II. During each term, three or four exercises in analysing a passage into clauses should be worked.

III. A few lessons on the growth of the language based on such books as Bradley, *Making of English*, and Weekley, *Romance of Words*, will arouse interest. This will also lead to appreciating the value of the etymological dictionary. If it is impossible to provide each pupil with a copy, two or three copies should be available in the room for reference. The *Concise Oxford Dictionary* will prove most suitable.

IV. Common errors in writing can be dealt with by using examples from the pupils' own compositions, and such quotations as may be found in *Punch* week by week. Stress should be laid on clearness of meaning, rather than on technical faults.

V. Parallels and comparisons with other languages learnt.

The Writing of English

It should no longer be necessary to give special time to the mechanical side of writing apart from corrections of compositions and other written work. The note-book must still be used for words incorrectly spelt, and for recording others looked up in the dictionary.

Use of Words

Exercises.

    i. Distinguish between words that are synonymous; e.g. *essential, needful.*

    ii. Collecting words relating to same subject. (The use of such a book as Roget's *Thesaurus* should be explained.)

    iii. Hackneyed expressions; e.g. *eagle eye.*

    iv. Single word for phrase; e.g. *admit as true, oriental market.*

    v. Prefixes and suffixes; e.g. *employee, employer*; *ante-room, antiseptic.*

    vi. Malapropisms; e.g. Dogberry's speeches in *Much Ado About Nothing.*

    vii. Definitions of given words with illustrations of uses; e.g. *navigable, wayward.*

    viii. Choosing most suitable word from a number of alternatives; e.g. 'Often had his (capricious, fitful) (imagination, fancy) dwelt on (visions, dreams) of (proper, personal) distinction'.

    ix. Criticism of journalese; e.g. 'He was made the recipient of a silver teapot'.

    x. Meanings of idioms and phrases; e.g. *the cap fits, Greek Kalends.*

    xi. Meanings of proverbs with stories to illustrate.

    xii. Criticism of 'commercial' English; e.g. 'Re yours of the 10th ult.'

Composition

I. *Note-making and Précis.* Considerable practice in these should be carried out, using school text-books, newspaper reports, and school lectures, as well as exercises in the English book.

II. *Paraphrasing.* Turning passages of archaic English into modern prose. Difficult passages from plays written in simpler language. Extracts used for this work should mainly depend for their interest on their content and not on their form, and there should be some value in getting the meaning expressed in a clearer fashion.

III. *Composition.* Lessons should be given on the following matters:

    i. Collecting ideas; use of sources such as books.

    ii. Arrangement and paragraphing.

    iii. Expression.

    iv. Opening sentences.

    v. The middle.

    vi. The end.

Subjects set should be as varied as possible. Each pupil should in the course of the year write one fairly long essay of each of the following types:

    i. Descriptive.
        E.g. Descriptions of pictures, buildings, people.

    ii. Narrative.
        E.g. Historical narrative, events witnessed, biographies.

    iii. Exposition.
        E.g. Accounts of experiments, model making, etc.

    iv. Argument.
        E.g. Speeches on debating society topics.

Other forms of exercise in writing:

i. Imaginative exercises in the form of diaries, letters, logs, play scenes, etc.

ii. Answers to questions set on books read.

iii. Translations from other languages into good English.

iv. The formal essay. Plenty of time should be given for preparation and a wide choice of subjects allowed.

v. Articles and reports for the class and school magazines.

The Reading of English.

Drama

Three long plays should be read, or several one-act plays substituted for one of these.

Suitable plays:

SHAKESPEARE.
  Tempest; Macbeth; Twelfth Night; Richard III; Coriolanus.

OTHER DRAMATISTS.
  Marlowe, *Doctor Faustus*; Jonson, *Every Man in His Humour*; Beaumont and Fletcher, *Knight of the Burning Pestle*; Sheridan, *School for Scandal.*

MODERN DRAMATISTS.
  Drinkwater, *Abraham Lincoln,* and *Oliver Cromwell*; Bernard Shaw, *Captain Brassbound's Conversion.*

ONE-ACT PLAYS.
  Galsworthy, *The Little Man*; Gilbert, *The Old Bull*; Maurice Baring, *Diminutive Dramas*; Brandane, *Rory Aforesaid.* (One of the many volumes of one-act plays now obtainable could be used.)

CLASSICAL DRAMA. (In translation.)
  Euripides, *Alcestis*; Sophocles, *Antigone*; Aristophanes, *The Birds.*

Before reading an Elizabethan play, a lesson should be given on the Playhouse, with sketches, or better still, by means of a model made in the school workshop. *The Knight of the Burning Pestle* will be found useful for making the Playhouse real to the pupils.

The method of treatment will be much as in the previous year, with the addition of one or two discussions on characters and plot. Such discussions should not begin by the teacher discoursing on the characters, but by eliciting from the pupils what traits have struck them in the course of the reading. Each characteristic mentioned should be illustrated by reference to the text.

The year might begin with the reading quickly of one or two one-act plays. This should be followed by the working out of a suitable plot for a play to be written by the class; a starting point may be found in a newspaper incident, a short story, or in the history work. When the idea has been accepted the class should be divided into groups to work out details and to settle on the characters. Each group might then be responsible for writing the first draft of the whole play. Discussion of these sketches will bring up many important points in play-structure and the use of dialogue. This work may have to be spread over more than one term, but its value cannot be exaggerated, as it forms a continuous exercise in the use of the imagination and in the writing of clear prose.

If a classical play is chosen, a lesson should be given on the conditions under which such plays were performed. Photographs of the ruins of theatres will help, and a clay model might be made.

Prose

The books chosen should make more demand on the pupils' attention than those read previously. The following may be suggested as suitable:

An anthology of Essays.
An anthology of Short Stories.
Boswell, *Tour of the Hebrides*.
Kinglake, *Eothen*.

Macaulay, *Essays*, such as 'Clive', 'Warren Hastings', 'Addison', and Chapter III of the *History of England*.

Thackeray, *English Humourists*.

Lamb, *Letters and Essays*.

Borrow, *Bible in Spain*.

Thoreau, *Walden*.

Carlyle, *On Heroes and Hero Worship*.

Burke, *American Speeches*.

Hazlitt, *Essays*.

Gibbon, Chapters I–III.

Ruskin, *Sesame and Lilies, Crown of Wild Olive*.

Stevenson, *Virginibus Puerisque*.

(For other suitable books, see library lists, pp. 98–100.)

Three books should be chosen as varied as possible in appeal. The bulk of the reading will be done silently in school, or at home. One of the books should be treated very thoroughly in class, and should be an introduction to a period, or a number of associated writers; the other books should only be used in class for the elucidation of difficulties encountered, and directional questions should be set which will help to concentrate the reader's attention on some definite lines of thinking.

Examples of Treatment

I. Hazlitt, *Essays*. For convenience the following scheme refers to Howe, *The Best of Hazlitt* (Methuen). The teacher should read Howe's *Life of Hazlitt* and the volume in the English Men of Letters series. The text may be read as an introduction to the prose writers of the French Revolution period in England; this study could be linked up with that of the poetry of the period as given in *The Golden Treasury*. (See next section.) Lessons should be given on the following topics, illustrated wherever possible with references to the *Essays*, by reproductions of photographs of the people mentioned, and by readings from the other writers and poets of the time. Such lessons should not be given as lectures but should be as conversational as possible; the aim is more to stimulate interest than to supply exhaustive information.

1. The life of Hazlitt.

2. The social life of his time.

3. His contemporaries: I. Lamb, De Quincey, Leigh Hunt.

4. His contemporaries: II. Wordsworth and Coleridge.

5. The character of Hazlitt as shown in his *Essays*.

These five lessons must be distributed through the term; intermediate lessons should be devoted to reading those Essays that bear on the previous lesson. An essay on Hazlitt could be set during the last weeks, not as a re-hash of the teacher's lessons but as giving the pupils' own impressions.

II. Thackeray, *English Humourists*. (Directional reading.) Apart from an introductory lesson on the general theme of the book, and a final period for class discussion, the teacher's part here is to encourage the pupils to read carefully with some definite object in view. It is not desirable that each pupil should have the same object as the others; sometimes it is possible to adapt these to individual tastes. At the end of the term one of the questions set might be answered on paper.

Specimen questions and themes

i. Before reading the book write down the titles of any books by the authors dealt with that you have read; at the end of your reading write down others you have read, or that you want to read if possible.

ii. What picture does Thackeray present of the Augustan Age?

iii. Which of the authors mentioned seems the most companionable?

   iv. How far does Thackeray illustrate his definition of 'the humourous writer' (*a*) in his own writing, and (*b*) in the work of the authors he lectured about?

   v. Justify, or object to, Thackeray's grouping of his authors.

   vi. Which of the authors appealed most strongly to Thackeray?

   vii. 'One gets from Thackeray the atmosphere rather than the apparatus of a period.' Is this statement borne out in *The English Humourists*?

   viii. Read Macaulay's 'Essay on Addison', and compare his views on Addison and Steele with those of Thackeray.

   ix. With which is Thackeray the more successful in his presentation, poets or prose writers?

   x. Illustrate from this book Thackeray's use of satire.

The Use of Books.

The pupils should be taught the use of an encyclopedia. They might also be shown the use of bibliographies (e.g. those of the National Book Council), library catalogues, and publishers' catalogues. A lesson on the history of a book from manuscript to publication is valuable. The school text-books (in all subjects) should also be used to illustrate the right use of such books.

Verse

The Golden Treasury will still prove the most serviceable anthology for this year. More attention should now be given to such subjects as metre, verse forms, etc. The following series of thirty lessons begins with a study of the Romantic poets, and would be suitable where such a book as Hazlitt's *Essays* is being read for prose. (See previous section.) If a prose text is taken from another period, the poets of the time should also be read as far as they are represented in *The Golden Treasury*. The two lessons on the old French forms have, in experience, proved useful for giving practice in verse making; there is a peculiar attraction in these forms, and the pupils will enjoy overcoming the technical difficulties they offer.

Reference numbers, as before, are to the edition containing Binyon's Fifth Book. A very brief biographical introduction should be given to each poet, and a portrait shown to the class.

1. Wordsworth's Nature Poetry. Some of these poems were read in the previous year; they should be recalled in order to get a fuller view of the subject. 222, 286, 288, 289, 301, 302, 305, 306, 323, 337.

2. Wordsworth's Sonnets. 254, 255, 256, 257, 326, 327. 255 should be learnt.

3. Lesson on metres. Coleridge's mnemonic lines should be learnt.

   Trochee trips from long to short,
   From long to long in solemn sort
   Slow Spondee stalks, strong foot, yet ill able
   Ever to come up with Dactyl trisyllable;
   Iambics march from short to long,
   With a leap and a bound the swift Anapaests throng.

4. Wordsworth's *Ode on Intimations of Immortality*. 338. Avoid making a paper scheme of this poem; reading aloud and discussion will suffice.

5. Speaking of verse, chosen by pupils.

6. Coleridge. 211, 316, 329. If *The Rime of the Ancient Mariner* is not familiar to the pupils, it should be read aloud to them.

7. Hood and Lamb. Hood: 268, 274, 279, 390; supplemented by the reading aloud of some of his humorous verse. Lamb: 264, 276, 282.

8. Byron. 212, 214, 216, 234, 246, 253, 266, 275. These will need supplementing with extracts from *Childe Harold's Pilgrimage*.

9. Shelley. 287, 321, 322, 339. Other poems should be read aloud, and also extracts from *Adonais* and *Prometheus Unbound*.

10. Blank Verse with special reference to the speaking of Shakespeare's verse; emphasise value of caesura.

11. Keats. A poet who always appeals to youth; little if any comment will be called for; the beauty of his poems should be allowed to make its own appeal. 209, 242, 272, 292.

12. The Odes of Keats; 290, 303, 328. Pictures of Grecian vases should be shown with 328, if possible the one reproduced in Colvin's *John Keats: His Life and Poetry*.

13. Speaking of blank verse.

14. Milton's *Lycidas*. 89.

15. Matthew Arnold. *Scholar-Gipsy* (385). The concluding simile should be learnt.

16. Matthew Arnold. 341, 427, 429, 444.

17. Forms of poetry; ballad, epic, lyric, ode, elegy, sonnet. Described where possible with reference to poems read previously. Rigid definitions are not desirable.

18. Speaking of verse.

19. Tennyson. 311, 356, 368, 406.

20. Tennyson. 384, 430, 432, 437, 445. These lessons should be supplemented by the reading of other poems by Tennyson, such as *Ulysses*.

21. Simile and metaphor. Illustrated by poems read. Pupils should hunt for further examples. It is not desirable, or useful, to teach pupils a list of over thirty 'figures of speech'.

22. Browning. 369, 373, 378, 394, 446. In spite of his difficulty, Browning is enjoyed by pupils of 15.

23. Swinburne. 365, 374, 377, 428, 439. The music of the verse is sufficient to capture the hearers.

24. French forms; Triolet and Rondeau. Examples of these, and of the Ballade will be found in my *Exercises in English*, pp. 135–6.

25. Speaking of verse; or reading aloud of Triolets.

26. French forms; the Ballade. See under 24th lesson.

27. Robert Bridges. 355, 362, 396. Supplemented lavishly by readings from his poems.

28. John Masefield. Represented by only one poem (400), but extracts from some of his long narrative poems should be read, especially *The Dauber* and *Reynard the Fox*.

29. Other living poets. Poems from the two volumes of *Poems of To-Day*, or from some other collection of modern verse, should be read to show the pupils that poetry is a living thing, and not merely of the past.

30. Speaking of favourite verse from *The Golden Treasury*.

One or two suggestions have been made above for poems to be learnt, but apart from these the pupils should be allowed to choose anything they like. Occasionally the poems so chosen should be read and not learnt until the pupils are word perfect; insistence on this too often 'kills' the music. The capacity for learning verse at this age varies considerably, and what would be easy work for one pupil may prove very difficult for another.

STAGE VI. FIFTH YEAR (*School Certificate Year*)

The syllabus for this year must be based on the requirements for the School Certificate Examination.

The English papers usually cover the following:

i. Essay (1 hour) with paraphrase, or précis, and sometimes analysis of sentences, with general questions on the use of words, errors in writing, etc.

ii. Literature: two or more of: a play by Shakespeare, set book of poetry (an anthology or selections from one poet), set prose authors (frequently including a novel).

iii. An alternative paper on General English Literature is sometimes possible.

The work to be done must be carefully planned by the teacher. It is desirable to spread the study of the books over the first two terms, leaving the third term for final reading, and for considerable practice in writing answers to questions. There should not be much need for oral teaching during that last term, as the pupils should concentrate on strengthening their weak places. This will call for individual attention.

i. *Essay, etc*. The choice of subjects set is fairly wide. The candidate needs practice particularly in

(*a*) picking his subject without waste of time; usually he should choose the subject he knows most about,

(*b*) writing a complete essay in the time given. It is most important that all essays written during this year should be done during the set time of the particular examination. During that time he has to

> choose a subject,
> jot down ideas,
> sort and arrange ideas,
> think of the development of the theme,
> get a good opening, and
> know what the end will be.

All this needs much practice, so that the candidate will know how much he can write in the given time, and adjust his material accordingly. Practice of this kind should begin with the first term.

Other matters that should be dealt with in lessons are:

openings,
study of good examples,
conclusions,

types of subjects and how to deal with them, e.g. discussion, abstract, historical, geographical.

Common errors in paragraphing, sentence structure, wording, etc., are best dealt with in essays written by the pupils, and if possible individually. Occasionally a good essay should be read aloud; bad ones should never be held up to criticism for the class. Paraphrasing and précis will also call for much practice; care must be taken to make use of varied material. (See Sections IV and V of my *Exercises in English*.) Note-making from text-books (for all subjects) should receive attention. A lesson should be given on how to get full benefit from such books. Passages that give trouble in set books should be freely used; such work helps to clear up difficulties.

Practice will also be needed in the writing of clear and succinct answers to questions not only for the other English papers, but for all subjects. It would be a good thing if the English teacher were to collaborate with other subject teachers and occasionally see answers that have been written for History, Geography and Science.

ii. *Literature*. The teacher must choose carefully which of the set books are to be used. Usually a Shakespeare play and a prose book are best; it is a pity to select a verse book for intensive study; for prose, a novel is sometimes possible, but unless it appeals strongly to the pupils, it will entail hard work for them; a comparatively short prose text is preferable because it is more amenable to special study.

The following suggestions cover most types.

(a) A play

The edition should not be overloaded with notes; they are apt to frighten the pupil! A 'plain text', on the other hand, almost invariably leads to too much time wasted in explanations by the teacher. A moderately annotated edition is most serviceable.

Method of treatment.

1. Reading aloud by teacher with no explanations.
2. Class- and home-reading by pupils; all difficulties not explained away by notes should be marked for oral explanation in class.

3. Play re-read, pupils taking parts in front of class.
4. Discussions on plot and characters. Notes should not be dictated, or the teacher's (often second-hand) opinions imposed on pupils. Suitable quotations in support of opinions should be given by pupils, so that text is always the basis of conclusions. Full freedom should be allowed the pupils in drawing their own conclusions.
5. Notable passages must be learnt.
6. Practice in context questions.
7. Practice in written answers.

(b) Verse

i. Poems by one author.
1. All poems should be read aloud by teacher.
2. Poems should be grouped according to subject or mood.
3. Study of metre.
4. Life of the poet, and his relationship with his period; illustrated by pictures, extracts from contemporary writers, etc.
5. Poems taken separately, read silently by pupils, and explanation of difficulties asked of teacher in class so that all benefit.
6. Summary of characteristics of poet, by means of suggestions from pupils supported with quotations.
7. Learning of well-known passages, and of passages the pupils like themselves. This is very important, as in the examination lavish quotation is a strong asset.
8. Practice in written answers.
9. Written appreciations.

ii. An anthology.
1. Reading aloud as before.
2. Grouping poems, first by subjects and moods, and then by authors.

3. Silent reading with opportunity of asking questions of teacher.

4. Short lives of poets; account of the period and conditions under which poems were written.

5. Summary of characteristics, and comparisons of treatment of similar themes.

6. Learning of typical passages and poems.

7. Practice in written answers.

8. Written appreciations.

(c) A novel

1. Home-reading by pupils.

2. Life of the novelist and account of his times.

3. Opportunity for asking explanation of difficulties.

4. Plot summary; a diagram is useful for bringing out structure.

5. Discussion of characters, with supporting quotations.

6. Final home-reading.

7. Oral questioning by teacher on plot and contexts.

8. Practice in written answers.

(d) A prose text (other than novel)

1. Home-reading; dictionary always at hand.

2. Life of writer and account of his times.

3. Summary of argument, or sequence of events.

4. Discussions on difficulties, etc.

5. Consideration of style and treatment.

6. Oral questions on contents.

7. Practice in written answers.

NOTE. Lessons on essay writing should be illustrated by reference to set books; e.g. paragraphing, arrangement of ideas, etc.

Where the teacher is more venturesome, the General Literature paper should be taken, provided

1. There is sufficient time available,
2. A good class library is at hand, with reference books, etc.

The method here will consist of a series of lessons by the teacher illustrated freely by extracts from authors dealt with, much home-reading by pupils, and discussions on what has been read.

This paper cannot be done by learning the contents of a history of literature; much reading is essential. Some of the wider-read pupils could easily take this paper with directional questions to guide them; but the normally little-read pupil should take the few set books.

STAGE VII. ADVANCED

Two groups of pupils must be considered:

A. Those taking English in the Higher School Certificate.

B. Those taking the H.S.C. but not taking English, and those who may be taking some other examination, or possibly no examination.

Both groups require practice in the writing of essays, etc.

A

The syllabus is designed to cover two years' work, and generally includes

I. Several plays by Shakespeare, sometimes two for detailed study and two for less detailed study;
II. Three or four set books;
III. Study of a period with set books; and,
IV. Sometimes, a knowledge of the historical development of the language.

These must be dealt with in turn.

I. *Shakespeare.*

All the plays set should be read through during the first four terms; the aim should be to get a thorough acquaintance with their contents. As far as possible the most important scenes at least should be read aloud, as this helps to fix the plot and ideas in the minds of the readers. The second reading should be done carefully to make sure that the meaning is grasped; a good annotated edition is useful for this, supplemented by the teacher dealing with individual difficulties raised by pupils. The third reading should be done with a view to finding material for answering questions and problems set beforehand. These questions should cover the whole field as far as possible and draw attention to important points.

The following, amongst others, might be set on *Hamlet*:

1. It has been said that two different versions are given of Horatio's antecedents: (*a*) that he is well acquainted with Denmark and its court and knew the late King well; (*b*) that he is not a native of Denmark, and is a stranger to the court. Trace these two versions through the play.

2. What evidence is there for thinking that the Queen was a guilty accomplice of Claudio?

3. Trace the relationship between Hamlet and Ophelia. Was he really in love with her, and if so, why did he treat her so harshly?

4. At what point in the play are the King's suspicions roused against Hamlet? Trace the development of these suspicions.

5. What impression does the character of Hamlet make on the other characters in the play?

6. Trace the waverings of Hamlet's resolution to revenge his father's murder.

Such questions are an aid to concentration, and in the course of collecting material the pupil adds considerably to his general knowledge of the text.

The next stage is the consideration of plot structure, and of characters; here again the assembling of the material should be done by the pupils.

When this course has been followed, the pupils should be advised to read some criticisms of the plays, and of Shakespeare's work.

The following will be found particularly stimulating:

J. Q. Adams, *A Life of William Shakespeare*.
Sir Walter Raleigh, *Shakespeare*.
Sir A. Quiller-Couch, *Shakespeare's Workmanship*.
Allardyce Nicoll, *Studies in Shakespeare*.
Granville Barker, *Studies in Shakespeare* (two series published).
A. C. Bradley, *Shakespearean Tragedy*.

It is assumed in the above scheme that a knowledge of the Elizabethan theatre has been gained in previous years; the reading of the plays with a knowledge of the contemporary background adds considerably to the interest and to the understanding.

Whenever possible the pupils should see performances of any of the plays they have to read; and if time permits, a performance by themselves will prove valuable.

The last term should be devoted mainly to practice in written answers and in questions on contexts.

II. *Set Books*.

The pupils should be able to study these without much 'teaching' Guidance on what to read, stimulating questions, and individual meeting of difficulties will be sufficient.

Occasionally a Chaucer text is set. Class-teaching will then be necessary on the language; and although the examination is only written, the pupils should also learn something of the correct pronunciation to derive full value from their work.

The same general method should be followed here as with the plays of Shakespeare; the pupils must first get a thorough knowledge of the text; once this has been obtained—largely by themselves—they are in a position to think out questions and problems; after their own thinking-out, they can be directed to the opinions and criticisms of other writers, but should be encouraged to adhere to their own opinions where these are supported by the text.

Frequent practice in answering questions and in contexts should be given, particularly during the last term.

III. *A Period of Literature.*

Several lessons should first be given on the period as a whole; main tendencies should be indicated; the social setting described, and the lives of the important writers given in so far as they bear on their work.

The most fruitful method here is that of frequent comparisons between the works of the different writers studied; style, method of treatment and ideas should all come up for review in this way.

It would be most advantageous if the same periods could be studied in History as in Literature; this linking-up of the work is important, and the teachers concerned should co-operate closely.

The writing of answers to questions must be frequently practised.

IV. *Language.*

The scope of the work is indicated by the books suggested by the various examining bodies. Such books as the following are generally given:

H. Bradley, *The Making of English.*
T. N. Toller, *The History of the English Language.*
The King's English.
H. Wyld, *Growth of English.*
Grattan and Gurrey, *Our Living Language.*
Jespersen, *Growth and Structure of the English Language.*

Definite lessons will have to be given for this work, based on the books recommended, supplemented by the teacher's own further knowledge. The subject is attractive, and with six terms for the syllabus, it should be possible to cover the ground thoroughly and with ease.

A AND B

Essay Work.

This is required for all candidates, and should be part of the work of those not taking the examination.

Lessons on such subjects as the following will be found helpful if illustrated freely from set books, and from the pupils' own reading:

Openings.	Narration.
Endings.	Exposition.
Paragraphing.	Argument.
Sequence of ideas.	Style.
Proportion.	Common errors in
Description.	word-order, etc.

A variety of questions on these and other matters will be found in my *Exercises in English.*

The oral discussion of the pupils' essays in class is most helpful.

One complete essay a month should be written under examination conditions, as so many candidates fail to proportion their work according to the allotted time.

B

Where no examination is in view, the teacher has a most delightful opportunity of stimulating interest in literature, and in expression. The following possibilities will illustrate the varied lines of study that could be followed according to the tastes and capabilities of the pupils themselves:

1. Training in thinking and method.

   Such books as the following would be suitable for reading:

   A. Wolf, *Essentials of Scientific Method.* (Allen and Unwin.)

   R. Thouless, *Straight and Crooked Thinking.* (Hodder.)

This subject would be of particular value with pupils who are specialising in Science.

2. A course of reading on one period of literature.

A suitable period would be the time of Johnson, and the reading might include:

> *A Shorter Boswell.* (Nelson, 1s. 9d.)
>
> Goldsmith, *Vicar of Wakefield*, *The Citizen of the World*, *She Stoops to Conquer*.
>
> Sir Joshua Reynolds, *Discourses on Art*.
>
> Johnson, *The Idler* (select essays), and one or two of the 'Lives'; e.g. Milton, Dryden, Swift, Addison, Pope, Gray.
>
> Gibbon, Chapters I–III; *Autobiography*.
>
> Sheridan, *The Rivals*, and *The School for Scandal*. –
>
> Fanny Burney, *Evelina*.
>
> Burke, *Speeches on America*, and *Reflections on the French Revolution*.
>
> Sterne, *Sentimental Journey*.

This list is already formidable in length, and could of course be extended to include Richardson and Fielding. The method of concentrating on one period, and of studying at the same time its history and customs, has proved most successful in developing a taste for good literature. There is something satisfactory in having covered one school of writing.

3. The reading of some books that demand considerable concentration of attention.

A few suitable books may be suggested:

> Burke, *Reflections on the French Revolution*. Read with Paine's *Rights of Man*.
>
> Ruskin, *Seven Lamps of Architecture*.
>
> Coleridge, *Biographia Literaria*, and Wordsworth's *Prelude*.

Many of the volumes in the Cambridge Manuals, and in the Home University Library are suitable for this type of work; for instance the volumes in the latter series on 'Political Thought in England' might be read.

Darwin, *The Origin of Species*.

Modern scientists offer a number of books that appeal to many older pupils; for instance the more popular writings of Andrade, Eddington and Jeans.

The method of discussion should be adopted in treating such books as these.

4. An introduction to the literature of another country (using translations). As example may be suggested a reading of some of the Icelandic sagas, many of which can be obtained at small cost. In Everyman's Library will be found

    Burnt Njal (Dasent), *Grettir Saga* (Hight), *Heimskringla* (Laing).

5. Some modern plays read, discussed and acted by the pupils.

    E.g. Shaw's *Arms and the Man*, Galsworthy's *Loyalties*, Barrie's *Dear Brutus*, Clemence Dane's *Will Shakespeare*, Barker's *Voysey Inheritance*.

6. The English short story.

    There are several anthologies available for such a study.

7. The English novel.

    A sketch of its development, and the reading of representative novels.

8. The Literature of the Bible.

    See Moulton's *How to read the Bible*.

9. Literature of Greece and Rome, using translations freely.

10. Development of the drama.

    Classical, English, French, etc.

11. Shakespearean investigation.

> Herford's *Sketch of recent Shakespearean Investigation* will supply a useful starting point.

12. The study of a long poem.

> *Iliad, Odyssey, Paradise Lost, Ring and the Book.*

One or two of these might be combined in such a way as to provide variety of subject and form.

In addition to such reading work, there should be more intensive study in the English language and its use. The possibility of a short course in the history of the language should be considered. For the written language, such a book as Fowler's *Modern English Usage* will be found valuable for suggestions. Some of the more important articles in that book should be studied carefully, and the pupils encouraged to look for further examples of incorrect usage in their own reading.

AIDS

I. CLASS AND SCHOOL MAGAZINES

The majority of schools now have their terminal magazines. Some of these are little more than records of events, matches, sports and other topical affairs. These should find their place in the magazine, but it is a pity if they form the bulk of the contents term after term. The magazine can be a means of stimulating those who have any marked ability to write articles on their interests, verse, short stories or light essays. In this way it can prove a useful aid to the teaching of English. The possibilities will be clearer if a list of contributions which appeared in one school magazine during some years be set down.

Extract from the Diary of Littlejohn.
Some thoughts on School Stories.
A Trip to Cambridge.
The Spectator visits the School.
Early Balloonists.
A Visit to Jersey.
Danton.
Men and Monkeys.
My First Shave.
An Election (after Malory).
The Gentle Elia.
A Pillow Fight. (Short story.)
From the Diary of a New Boy.
Meditations in the Geography Room. (Verse.)
A Narrow Escape. (Story.)
A House Match. (Verse.)
A composite story. (Each of three writers handed on his section without comment to the next; a fourth finished the story.)
London—In January. (Verse.)
The Fog.
To a Worn-out Mackintosh. (Verse.)

A Bullfight.
Sonnets: War; Spring.
The Chess-player's Soliloquy. (A Browning parody.)

The above list will be sufficient to indicate the possibilities for original writing if the school magazine is used, as it should be, for the encouragement of those pupils who have imagination and the power of expression.

It should be added that school magazines should invariably be run entirely by the pupils; the editing, the business arrangements, and the reporting of events should be their work. It may be necessary to have a member of the Staff as censor.

Class magazines are also to be encouraged. It is not essential that these should be printed or duplicated. Perhaps it would be more correct to call them class Commonplace Books. A stiff clip file, the outside decorated, should be used, and manuscript contributions put into it, with sketches, drawings and any other items that may prove suitable. The class itself should vote which attempts are worthy of inclusion in this gallery. It is a simple matter to arrange for each pupil to take the magazine home with him, so that there may be an added inducement to reach the required standard of the class approval.

II. SCHOOL SOCIETIES

Literary, Debating and Dramatic Societies can be aids to the raising of the standard of English work. Unfortunately they are usually confined to the older pupils, sometimes by rule, and in actual practice by the fact that a junior pupil will seldom take an active part in an affair with seniors. It is therefore desirable that societies for pupils of the middle forms should be organised so that they too can reap the benefits of these activities. As far as possible the organisation should be done by the members themselves. In the middle forms perhaps it may be necessary for a teacher to act as guide, and occasionally as chairman of debates.

It is not easy to find new suitable subjects for general debates; the well-worn ones are only well-worn to the teacher and not to the pupils; care, however, should be taken to see that the same subject is not repeated too frequently. The subjects chosen should admit of general debate; there should be definitely conflict of opinion, otherwise the debate may lapse into dull speeches mostly in favour of one side. A pleasant variation of the set subject is to have an impromptu debate, when a number of subjects, some facetious, are taken at random and a short time devoted to each. This often gives an opportunity for the shy member to gain courage. We can all probably remember our first attempt at speaking in public; the nervousness that seized us before getting on our feet, and the deep seriousness of our contribution to the discussion; a contribution that in my case fell flat! It is important that we should help the nervous boy who would like to speak and encourage him as much as we can; it may also be necessary to suppress at times the verbose speaker.

Some schools organise with considerable success a Parliament; few forms of debate are more valuable in a school, for apart from providing a play-acting element that tends to stimulate the speakers, the mock Parliament offers more varied opportunities for speaking. It also has a value in providing a training in disciplined debate, and in teaching a knowledge of procedure. Other experiments that should be tried are the Town Council, a League of Nations Assembly, and the mock Trial.

The Literary Society is best restricted to older pupils who have a certain amount of reading behind them; lectures, discussions, and the reading of short papers are useful activities. The History Society, and the various scientific societies will make appeal to other pupils, and are to be encouraged.

School dramatic clubs can do most valuable work if organised carefully. To reap the greatest benefit from them it is essential that the amount of time spent on one production should be as short as possible. If too high a standard of result is set, few pupils will be able to take part. It is difficult to describe the desirable standard; perhaps it is sufficient to say that the producer should concentrate his attention on clear speaking rather than on the niceties of movement. Nor should too much attention be given to such matters as dress and setting; there should be as much improvisation of properties and scenery as possible. The latter should only be used if it provides a useful form of expression for the pupils of artistic ability.

A dramatic club should not only produce plays for acting on the platform, but should also arrange for play-readings. The difficulty of obtaining sufficient copies for those taking part can be overcome by the school joining the British Drama League. Parts should be allotted in rotation irrespective of whether the reader is good or not; the poor readers need the practice more than the good ones. If the copies are given out some days beforehand even the worst reader will make a fair attempt, and having once managed to get through his part he will gain confidence and soon improve. If 'star' parts are always given to 'star' readers the educational value of the work will be unduly restricted.

There is no reason to limit such reading clubs to the drama; the short story, the essay, and other forms of literature can be used in the same way with profit.

III. LIBRARIES

Large sums of money are often provided to equip laboratories and workshops, and to supply the necessary apparatus for experiments, but too often there is very little money to be had for school libraries. It is possible to find the cash for a delicate piece of electrical apparatus that may cost a sum of money large enough to make the English teacher happy for many months. Yet if he were rashly to ask for a copy of the *New English Dictionary* at the price of £63, he would probably be refused, although the purchase would be for a generation.

Every school should have its general library, and for the first five Stages of the course each class should have a small collection of books. After that, the school library should be available for a more varied supply of literature. The first requirement for the school library is a room set apart for one purpose only—as a library, not as a spare class-room. It should be well lighted and comfortable so that pupils feel that it is a pleasure to go there. If practicable, there should always be someone in attendance to give help in finding books, or to suggest suitable reading for any definite purpose. There should be ample opportunity for browsing; forced taste will never lead to true appreciation. There is much wisdom in Charles Lamb's note about his sister: 'She was tumbled early, by accident or design, into a spacious closet of good old English reading, without much selection or prohibition, and browsed at will upon that fair and wholesome pasturage. Had I twenty girls, they should be brought up in this fashion'. Once interest has been roused in a subject or a type of writing, it will inevitably lead on to something else. It will be in miniature the story of the man who looked into the British Museum one day to verify a minor point in history, and spent the rest of his leisure there collecting material for an authoritative work on the period.

There should be a good reference section to the library. Such a selection as the following would serve many purposes:

An Etymological Dictionary of Modern English. Weekley. (Murray, £2. 2s.)
Dictionary of English Usage. H. W. Fowler. (Oxford, 7s. 6d.)
Chambers's Encyclopedia. (£10.) This is the most useful encyclopedia for the general reader.
Concise Dictionary of National Biography. (Oxford, 21s.)
Classical Dictionary. Smith. (Murray, 21s.)
Thesaurus. Roget. (Longmans, 7s. 6d.)
A Dictionary of Phrase and Fable. Brewer. (Cassell, 25s.)
Gazetteer of the World. (Chambers, 15s.)
Shakespeare Glossary. Onions. (Oxford, 5s.)
The Statesman's Year Book. (Macmillan, £1.)
Record Atlas. (Philip, 10s. 6d.)

Latin, French and German Dictionaries.
Books to Read. (The Library Association, 10*s.*)
Bradshaw's Time Tables.

Senior classes should be taken to the library occasionally
to have some instruction in the use of books and how to
find information.

Class libraries are as important as a school library. It
has been indicated in the syllabus that in addition to the
books chosen for lesson reading there should be a stock
of other books suited to the age of the class, for leisure-
time reading. This does not necessitate a large outlay.
Forty volumes will provide sufficient variety for a year in
a class of twenty-five pupils. There are now available so
many well-produced and low-priced editions that the
complete collection could be bought for a few pounds. It
is important to emphasise the need for variety in selecting
the books for this small library; an attempt should be
made to appeal to many tastes, to the pupil who is fond of
the open air, to the one interested in history, to the
scientific pupil and the one who has a passion for the
mechanical. Such a selection necessarily goes beyond the
bounds of a strictly literary collection, but this is inevitable
if varied interests are to be captured.

A small reference section should be included. The
following would make a good beginning:

Smaller Classical Dictionary. Smith. (Everyman, 2*s.*) (Or
      better, the library binding at 3*s.*)
Dictionary of Non-classical Mythology. (Everyman, 2*s.*; 3*s.*)
Concise Oxford Dictionary. (Oxford, 7*s.* 6*d.*)
Handy Reference Atlas. (Bartholomew, 12*s.* 6*d.*)
Whitaker's Almanack. (6*s.*)
Language Dictionaries.

The pupils should be taught how to use these books,
and be encouraged to refer to them during reading rather
than to the teacher.

The following lists of suitable books for each of the
first five Stages will indicate the possible scope of class

libraries. It is clearly impossible to include in a small collection of books all the desirable volumes; the chief principle of selection has been the need for appealing to many different interests in the hope that the readers may be encouraged to go farther in the pursuit of their own particular fancies. Titles of books already suggested in the syllabus are not repeated.

STAGES I AND II

General Literature and Poetry

Frazer, Lady. *Leaves from 'The Golden Bough'*. (Macmillan, 10*s*. 6*d*.)

Buckley, E. F. *Children of the Dawn*. (Wells Gardner, 7*s*. 6*d*.)

Baldwin, James. *The Story of Roland*. (Harrap, 2*s*. 6*d*.)

Gilbert, Henry. *Robin Hood*. (Nelson, 6*s*.)

Macaulay, M. C. *Stories re-told from 'The Canterbury Tales'*. (Cambridge, 2*s*. 9*d*.)

Steele Smith, M. *Stories from Spenser*. (Cambridge, 3*s*.)

Herbertson, A. G. *Heroic Legends*. (Blackie, 7*s*. 6*d*.)

Steele, F. A. *English Fairy Tales*. (Macmillan, 7*s*. 6*d*.)

Milne, A. A. *When We Were Very Young*. (Methuen, 7*s*. 6*d*.)

Stevenson, R. L. *A Child's Garden of Verses*. (Heinemann, 2*s*. 6*d*.)

Bain, A. Watson (editor). *A Poetry Book for Children*. (Cambridge, 2*s*. 6*d*.)

De la Mare, Walter (editor). *Come hither: a Collection of Rhymes and Poems for the Young of all Ages*. (Constable, 10*s*. 6*d*.)

Carroll, Lewis. *The Hunting of the Snark*. (Macmillan, 2*s*.)

Science and Hobbies

Lewis, I. M. *Astronomy for Young Folk*. (Hutchinson, 7*s*. 6*d*.)

Woodward, Marcus. *Camp Fire Nature Yarns*. (Pearson, 2*s*. 6*d*.)

Batten, H. Mortimer. *Dramas of the Wild Folk*. (Partridge, 3*s*. 6*d*.)

Budden, John. *Jungle John: a Book of the Big Game Jungles*. (Longmans, 6*s*.)

Golding, Harry (editor). *The Wonder Book of Pets.* (Ward, Lock, 6s.)
Barnard, John (editor). *The Handy Boy's Book.* (Ward, Lock, 6s.)

Biography and History, including Exploration

Hall, Harry R. *Days before History.* (Harrap, 2s.)
Masefield, John. *A Book of Discoveries.* (Wells Gardner, 7s. 6d.)
Van Loon, Hendrik. *The Story of Mankind.* (Harrap, 7s. 6d.)
Bridges, T. C. *The Book of Discovery.* (Harrap, 7s. 6d.)
Hayward, Arthur L. *The Boys' Book of Explorers.* (Cassell, 5s.)
Binyon, Mrs Laurence. *Heroes in History.* (Frowde, 2s. 6d.)
Power, E. and R. *Boys and Girls of History.* (Cambridge, 7s. 6d.)
Mathews, Basil. *Livingstone the Pathfinder.* (Oxford, 2s. 6d.)

Fiction

Ballantyne, R. M. *The Coral Island.* (Nelson, 1s. 6d.)
Barrie, Sir James M. *Peter Pan and Wendy.* (Hodder, 2s. 6d.)
Dawson, A. J. *Finn, the Wolfhound.* (Richards, 6s.)
Doyle, Sir A. Conan. *Sir Nigel.* (Murray, 2s.)
—— *The White Company.* (Murray, 2s.)
Fitzpatrick, Sir James P. *Jock of the Bushveld.* (Longmans, 5s.)
Grahame, Kenneth. *The Golden Age.* (Nelson, 2s. 6d.)
—— *Dream Days.* (Nelson, 2s. 6d.)
—— *The Wind in the Willows.* (Methuen, 3s. 6d.)
Kipling, Rudyard. *Puck of Pook's Hill.* (Macmillan, 6s.)
—— *Rewards and Fairies.* (Macmillan, 6s.)
—— *The Jungle Books.* (Macmillan, 6s.)
—— *Just So Stories.* (Macmillan, 6s.)
Lofting, Hugh. *The Story of Dr Dolittle.* (Cape, 3s. 6d.)
MacDonald, George. *At the Back of the North Wind.* (Blackie, 5s.)
Masefield. *Jim Davis.* (Wells Gardner, 2s. 6d.)
Milne, A. A. *Winnie-the-pooh.* (Methuen, 7s. 6d.)
Stevenson, R. L. *Treasure Island.* (Heinemann, 2s. 6d.)
Twain, Mark. *The Adventures of Tom Sawyer.* (Harrap, 2s. 6d.)
Wyss, J. R. *The Swiss Family Robinson.* (Black, 3s. 6d.)
Yonge, Charlotte M. *The Lances of Lynwood.* (Macmillan, 2s. 6d.)

Stage III

General Literature and Poetry

Bulfinch, Thomas. *The Age of Fable*. (Dent, 2s.)
Wilson, Romer. *Green Magic*. (Cape, 7s. 6d.)
Guerber, H. A. *The Myths of Greece and Rome*. (Harrap, 10s. 6d.)
—— *Myths of the Norsemen*. (Harrap, 10s. 6d.)
Stephens, James. *Irish Fairy Tales*. (Macmillan, 6s.)
Lang, Andrew. *Tales of Troy and Greece*. (Longmans, 5s.)
Knowles, Sir James. *The Legends of King Arthur*. (Warne, 6s.)
De la Mare, Walter. *Peacock Pie: a Book of Rhymes*. (Constable, 4s. 6d.)
Chisholm, Louey (editor). *The Golden Staircase*. (Jack, 10s. 6d.)
Grahame, Kenneth (editor). *The Cambridge Book of Poetry for Children*. (Cambridge, 5s.)
Reynolds, E. E. (editor). *Twenty-two Story Poems*. (Harrap, 2s.)
Lear, Edward, etc. *A Book of Nonsense*. (Dent, 2s.)

Science and Hobbies

Gibson, Charles R. *The Stars and their Mysteries*. (Seeley, 5s.)
McDougall, A. L. *Nature's Mystic Movements*. (Pitman, 2s. 6d.)
Duncan, F. Martin and Lucy T. *The Book of the Countryside*. (Collins, 5s.)
Batten, H. Mortimer. *Romances of the Wild*. (Blackie, 5s.)
Seton, E. Thompson. *Two Little Savages*. (Constable, 7s. 6d.)
Williams, Archibald. *How it is Made*. (Nelson, 5s.)
Hawks, Ellison. *The Book of Electrical Wonders*. (Harrap, 7s. 6d.)
Jackson, G. Gibbard. *Hobbies for Boys*. (Low, 6s.)
James, S. T. *The Railwayman*. (Nelson, 6s.)

Biography and History, including Exploration

Quennell, M. and C. H. B. Everyday Life Series. (Batsford, 5s. each.)
—— *History of Everyday Things in England*. (Batsford, 2 vols., 8s. 6d. each.)
Happold, F. C. *The Adventure of Man*. (Christophers, 4s. 6d.)

Archer, Arthur B. *Stories of Exploration and Discovery*. (Cambridge, 3*s.*)
Bridges, T. C. and Tiltman, H. H. *Heroes of Modern Adventure*. (Harrap, 7*s.* 6*d.*)
Hedin, Sven. *From Pole to Pole*. (Macmillan, 10*s.*)
Quiller-Couch, Sir A. T. *The Roll Call of Honour*. (Nelson, 1*s.* 9*d.*)
Lang, Mrs Andrew. *The Red Book of Heroes*. (Longmans, 5*s.*)
Strang, Herbert (editor). *Pioneers of Canada*. (Oxford, 3*s.* 6*d.*)
Scott, G. Firth. *The Romance of Polar Exploration*. (Seeley, 6*s.*)

Fiction

Baker, Sir Samuel W. *Cast Up by the Sea*. (Macmillan, 3*s.* 6*d.*)
Ballantyne, R. M. *Ungava*. (Nelson, 3*s.* 6*d.*)
Buchan, John. *Prester John*. (Nelson, 2*s.* 6*d.*)
Bunyan, John. *The Pilgrim's Progress*. (Nelson, 1*s.* 6*d.*)
Cooper, James Fenimore. *Last of the Mohicans*. (Macmillan, 3*s.* 6*d.*)
Crockett, S. R. *The Raiders*. (Nash, 2*s.* 6*d.*)
Dickens, Charles. *David Copperfield*. (Dent, 2*s.*)
Doyle, Sir A. Conan. *Uncle Bernac*. (Murray, 2*s.* 6*d.*)
Falkner, John Meade. *Moonfleet*. (Arnold, 2*s.* 6*d.*)
Freeman, R. Austin. *The Unwilling Adventurer*. (Hodder, 2*s.* 6*d.*)
Haggard, Sir H. Rider. *King Solomon's Mines*. (Cassell, 2*s.* 6*d.*)
Hughes, Thomas. *Tom Brown's Schooldays*. (Nelson, 1*s.* 6*d.*)
Jefferies, Richard. *Bevis*. (Dent, 2*s.*)
Marryat, Captain Frederick. *Mr Midshipman Easy*. (Nelson, 1*s.* 6*d.*)
Morris, William. *A Dream of John Ball*. (Longmans, 3*s.* 6*d.*)
Quiller-Couch, Sir A. T. *The Splendid Spur*. (Dent, 3*s.* 6*d.*)
Wells, H. G. *The First Men in the Moon*. (Collins, 2*s.* 6*d.*)
Weyman, Stanley J. *The Red Cockade*. (Murray, 2*s.* 6*d.*)
—— *Under the Red Robe*. (Murray, 2*s.* 6*d.*)

STAGE IV

General Literature and Poetry

Scott, Sir Walter. *Poetical Works*. (Macmillan, 4*s.* 6*d.*)
Henley, William E. (editor). *Lyra Heroica*. (Macmillan, 3*s.* 6*d.*)
Meynell, Alice (editor). *The School of Poetry*. (Collins, 3*s.* 6*d.*)

Fowler, Ethel L. (editor). *For Your Delight*. (Poetry Bookshop, 2s. 6d.)
Macaulay, Lord. *Lays of Ancient Rom.* (Nelson, 1s. 6d.)
Morris, William. *Life and Death of Jason*. (Longmans, 3s. 6d.)
Methuen, Sir Algernon (editor). *An Anthology of Modern Verse*. (Methuen, 6s.)
Masefield, John. *Dauber*. (Heinemann, 3s. 6d.)
Belloc, Hilaire. *A Picked Company*. (Methuen, 3s. 6d.)
Gardiner, A. G. *Leaves in the Wind*. (Dent, 1s. 6d.)
Hazlitt, William. *Twenty-two Essays*. (Harrap, 2s. 6d.)
Lucas, E. V. (editor). *The Gentlest Art*. (Methuen, 3s. 6d.)
Rhys, Ernest (editor). *A Century of Essays*. (Dent, 2s.)
Reynolds, E. E. (editor). *The Shorter Lamb*. (Nelson, 1s. 9d.)
Bailey, John (editor). *The Shorter Boswell*. (Nelson, 1s. 9d.)

Science and Hobbies

Gregory, Sir Richard A. *The Vault of Heaven*. (Methuen, 6s.)
Grew, E. S. *The Romance of Modern Geology*. (Seeley, 6s.)
Westell, W. P. *The Boy's Own Nature Book*. (R.T.S., 6s.)
Stopes, Marie C. *The Study of Plant Life*. (Blackie, 6s.)
Grenfell, Sir Wilfred T. *Yourself and Your Body*. (Hodder, 3s. 6d.)
Greenly, Henry. *Model Engineering*. (Cassell, 8s. 6d.)
Bacon, Admiral Sir Reginald. *A Simple Guide to Wireless*. (Mills and Boon, 3s. 6d.)
Fayers, Martin A. *A Handbook for Young Gardeners*. (Oxford, 2s. 6d.)
Bridges, T. C. *A Book of the Sea*. (Harrap, 7s. 6d.)
Jones, Bernard E. *Every Boy His Own Mechanic*. (Cassell, 5s.)
Walker, Allen S. *The Romance of Building*. (Philip, 3s. 6d.)

Biography and History, including Exploration

Henderson, Keith. *Prehistoric Man*. (Harrap, 7s. 6d.)
Niver, H. B. *A Brief Story of the World*. (Harrap, 3s. 6d.)
Dorling, H. Taprell. *Sea Venturers of Britain*. (Collins, 2s. 6d.)
Hakluyt, Richard. *A Selection of the Principal Voyages*. (Heinemann, 6s.)
Buchan, John. *Sir Walter Raleigh*. (Nelson, 1s. 9d.)
Lee, Sir Sidney. *Great Englishmen of the XVIth Century*. (Harrap, 3s. 6d.)

Southey, Robert. *Life of Nelson*. (Macmillan, 3s.)
Benson, E. F. *Sir Francis Drake*. (Lane, 12s. 6d.)
Ponsonby, Arthur and Dorothea. *Rebels and Reformers*. (Allen and Unwin, 2s. 6d.)
Yonge, Charlotte M. *A Book of Golden Deeds*. (Blackie, 2s.)
Buchan, John. *A Book of Escapes and Hurried Journeys*. (Nelson, 2s. 6d.)
Newbolt, Sir Henry. *The Book of the Long Trail*. (Longmans, 5s.)
Sanderson, Edgar. *Stories of Great Pioneers*. (Seeley, 3s. 6d.)
Younghusband, Sir Francis. *The Epic of Mount Everest*. (Arnold, 7s. 6d.)
Evans, Edward R. G. R. *South with Scott*. (Collins, 2s. 6d.)
Shackleton, Sir Ernest H. *South*. (Heinemann, 5s.)

Fiction

Buchan, John. *John Burnet of Barns*. (Lane, 3s. 6d.)
—— *The Path of the King*. (Hodder, 3s. 6d.)
Churchill, Winston. *Richard Carvel*. (Macmillan, 5s.)
Crockett, S. R. *The Black Douglas*. (Dent, 1s. 6d.)
Dickens, Charles. *Oliver Twist*. (Nelson, 1s. 6d.)
—— *The Pickwick Papers*. (Nelson, 1s. 6d.)
Doyle, Sir A. Conan. *Micah Clarke*. (Harrap, 2s. 6d.)
Dumas, Alexandre. *The Three Musketeers*. (Nelson, 1s. 6d.)
Hope, Anthony. *The Prisoner of Zenda*. (Arrowsmith, 3s. 6d.)
Johnston, Mary. *By Order of the Company*. (Butterworth, 2s. 6d.)
Kipling, Rudyard. *Kim*. (Macmillan, 6s.)
London, Jack. *White Fang*. (Methuen, 2s. 6d.)
Lytton, Lord. *The Last of the Barons*. (Dent, 2s.)
Mason, A. E. W. *The Courtship of Morrice Buckler*. (Nash, 2s. 6d.)
Melville, Herman. *Moby Dick*. (Low, 2s. 6d.)
Munro, Neil. *The New Road*. (Blackwood, 3s. 6d.)
Parker, Sir Gilbert. *The Seats of the Mighty*. (Harrap, 3s. 6d.)
Russell, William Clark. *The Wreck of the* Grosvenor. (Low, 2s. 6d.)
Scott, Sir Walter. *Woodstock*. (Dent, 2s.)
—— *Ivanhoe*. (Dent, 2s.)
—— *Quentin Durward*. (Dent, 2s.)
Stephens, James. *The Crock of Gold*. (Macmillan, 2s. 6d.)

Stevenson, R. L. *The Master of Ballantrae*. (Heinemann, 2*s.* 6*d.*)
Thackeray, W. M. *The History of Henry Esmond*. (Nelson, 1*s.* 6*d.*)
Wells, H. G. *The Invisible Man*. (Collins, 2*s.* 6*d.*)
Weyman, Stanley J. *The House of the Wolf*. (Nelson, 1*s.* 6*d.*)
White, Stewart Edward. *The Blazed Trail*. (Constable, 3*s.* 6*d.*)

STAGE V

General Literature and Poetry

Noyes, Alfred. *Ballads and Poems*. (Blackwood, 7*s.* 6*d.*)
Quiller-Couch, Sir A. T. (editor). *The Oxford Book of English Verse*. (Oxford, 8*s.* 6*d.*)
—— *The Oxford Book of English Prose*. (Oxford, 8*s.* 6*d.*)
Methuen, Sir Algernon (editor). *Shakespeare to Hardy*. (Methuen, 6*s.*)
Squire, J. C. (compiler). *Selections from Modern Poets*. (Secker, 2*s.* 6*d.*)
Poems of To-day. Two series. (Sidgwick, 3*s.* 6*d.* each.)
Carlyle, Thomas. *On Heroes, etc.* (Cambridge, 2*s.* 6*d.*)
Peacock, W. (editor). *Selected English Essays*. (Oxford, 2*s.*)
Pritchard, F. H. (editor). *Essays of To-day*. (Harrap, 3*s.* 6*d.*)
Lynd, Robert. *Selected Essays*. (Dent, 1*s.*)
Bailey, John. *Dr Johnson and His Circle*. (Butterworth, 2*s.* 6*d.*)
Belloc, Hilaire. *The Path to Rome*. (Nelson, 2*s.* 6*d.*)
Pepys, Samuel. *Everybody's Pepys*. (Bell, 10*s.* 6*d.*)
Stevenson, R. L. *Virginibus Puerisque*. (Macmillan, 1*s.* 9*d.*)
Taylor, Hedley V. (editor). *Letters of Great Writers*. (Blackie, 2*s.* 6*d.*)
Squire, J. C. (editor). *The Comic Muse*. (Collins, 2*s.* 6*d.*)
Masefield, John. *Collected Poems*. (Heinemann, 8*s.* 6*d.*)

Science and Hobbies

Ball, Sir Robert S. *The Story of the Heavens*. (Cassell, 15*s.*)
Bragg, Sir William. *The World of Sound*. (Bell, 6*s.*)
Martin, Geoffrey. *Triumphs and Wonders of Modern Chemistry*. (Low, 7*s.* 6*d.*)
Smith, B. Webster. *The World in the Past*. (Warne, 10*s.* 6*d.*)

Furneaux, W. S. *The Out-door World.* (Longmans, 6s. 6d.)

Jefferies, Richard. *The Gamekeeper at Home.* (Collins, 2s.)

Bragg, Sir William. *Old Trades and New Knowledge.* (Bell, 8s. 6d.)

Morgan, A. P. and Sims, J. W. *The Boy Electrician.* (Harrap, 7s. 6d.)

Bridges, T. C. and Tiltman, H. H. *Master Minds of Modern Science.* (Harrap, 7s. 6d.)

Allen, Cecil J. *Railways of To-day.* (Warne, 12s. 6d.)

Goodyear, Frederick. *Printing and Bookcrafts.* (Harrap, 10s. 6d.)

Biography and History, including Exploration

Lodge, Sir Oliver. *Pioneers of Science.* (Macmillan, 7s. 6d.)

Trevelyan, Sir George O. *The Life and Letters of Lord Macaulay.* (Longmans, 2 vols., 6s. each.)

Balfour, Sir Graham. *Life of Robert Louis Stevenson.* (Methuen, 2s. 6d.)

Gwynn, S. *Captain Scott.* (Lane, 12s. 6d.)

Blore, G. H. *Victorian Worthies.* (Oxford, 7s. 6d.)

Brendon, J. A. *Great Navigators and Discoverers.* (Harrap, 7s. 6d.)

Tristram, W. Outram. *Coaching Days and Coaching Ways.* (Macmillan, 3s. 6d.)

Noel, J. B. L. *Through Tibet to Everest.* (Arnold, 10s. 6d.)

Scott, Robert F. *Scott's Last Expedition.* (Murray, 7s. 6d.)

—— *The Voyage of the* Discovery. (Murray, 7s. 6d.)

Beebe, William. *The Edge of the Jungle.* (Witherby, 12s. 6d.)

Prescott, William H. *The Conquest of Mexico.* (Oxford, 2 vols., 2s. each.)

Butler, Sir William F. *The Great Lone Land.* (Burns and Oates, 5s.)

Morris, G. W. and Wood, L. S. *The English-speaking Nations.* (Oxford, 3s. 6d.)

—— *The Golden Fleece.* (Oxford, 3s. 6d.)

Jones, Robert and Sherman, S. S. *The League of Nations.* (Pitman, 5s.)

Bullen, Frank T. *The Cruise of the* Cachelot. (Murray, 2s. 6d.)

Fiction

Benson, E. F. *David Blaize.* (Hodder, 3s. 6d.)

Blackmore, R. D. *Lorna Doone.* (Low, 2s. 6d.)

Bone, David William. *The Brassbounder*. (Duckworth, 3s. 6d.)
Bowen, Marjorie. *The Governor of England*. (Methuen, 3s. 6d.)
Buchan, John. *Huntingtower*. (Hodder, 3s. 6d.)
Butler, Samuel. *Erewhon*. (Cape, 3s. 6d.)
Dickens, Charles. *Martin Chuzzlewit*. (Nelson, 1s. 6d.)
Eliot, George. *Adam Bede*. (Nelson, 1s. 6d.)
English Short Stories. (Dent, 2s.)
Hardy, Thomas. *The Trumpet-Major*. (Macmillan, 6s.)
—— *Under the Greenwood Tree*. (Macmillan, 6s.)
Hewlett, Maurice. *The Forest Lovers*. (Macmillan, 3s. 6d.)
—— *Richard Yea-and-Nay*. (Macmillan, 3s. 6d.)
Johnston, Mary. *Lewis Rand*. (Butterworth, 2s. 6d.)
Lytton, Lord. *The Last Days of Pompeii*. (Harrap, 2s. 6d.)
Merriman, Henry Seton. *In Kedar's Tents*. (Murray, 3s. 6d.)
Mitchison, Naomi. *The Conquered*. (Cape, 3s. 6d.)
Newbolt, Sir Henry. *The Old Country*. (Murray, 7s. 6d.)
Parker, Sir Gilbert. *The Battle of the Strong*. (Harrap, 3s. 6d.)
Phillpotts, Eden. *Storm in a Teacup*. (Hutchinson, 3s. 6d.)
Poe, Edgar Allan. *Tales of Mystery and Imagination*. (Dent, 2s.)
Reade, Charles. *The Cloister and the Hearth*. (Nelson, 1s. 6d.)
Roberts, Charles G. D. *The Forge in the Forest*. (Dent, 4s. 6d.)
Scott, Sir Walter. *The Antiquary*. (Black, 2s. 6d.)
—— *Old Mortality*. (Black, 2s. 6d.)
—— *Rob Roy*. (Black, 2s. 6d.)
Thackeray, W. M. *Vanity Fair*. (Nelson, 1s. 6d.)
Wells, H. G. *The History of Mr Polly*. (Collins, 2s. 6d.)
—— *Kipps*. (Collins, 2s. 6d.)
—— *Tono-Bungay*. (Collins, 2s. 6d.)
Weyman, Stanley J. *Ovington's Bank*. (Murray, 3s. 6d.)
Williamson, Henry. *Tarka the Otter*. (Putnam, 3s. 6d.)

IV. FOR THE TEACHER

The best aid for the teacher is his own reading and writing. No one can be an inspiring teacher of English unless he reads widely, and also practises the art of writing. The need for the latter is too often overlooked. There are various ways in which the teacher's own ability to write can be cultivated: the keeping of a diary, the writing of comments on books read, an occasional formal essay, or an attempt in the lighter manner of the third leaders in *The Times*. All these will help to keep the difficulties of writing fresh, so that he can the more convincingly teach.

A teacher of English should not confine himself in his reading to books bearing on his work, but keep in touch as far as possible with all modern literature. This is a vast undertaking at first sight when it is considered that some 12,000 books are published annually. Guidance is obtainable from several sources; the lists published by the National Book Council (to which the teacher should belong) are helpful, and such weekly periodicals as *The Times Literary Supplement* make it a simple matter to weed out 90 per cent. of the books published. It would need a private fortune to buy even a small proportion of the books that should be read. There are various circulating libraries available, and the National Central Library, which works in collaboration with local libraries, can be of great assistance. The gentle art of 'skipping' should be cultivated.

Apart from general reading there are some books that will prove of special help in the teaching of English. I mention here those that I have myself found of particular value.

The Teaching of English

English for the English. George Sampson. (Cambridge, 2s. 6d.)
The Rudiments of Criticism. E. A. Greening-Lambourn. (Oxford, 2s. 6d.)
The Teaching of English. W. S. Tomkinson. (Oxford, 6s.)
Aims and Methods in the Teaching of English. Arnold Smith. (Constable, 2s. 6d.)
Inspirational Teaching. G. Mackaness. (Dent, 10s. 6d.)
The Play Way. H. Caldwell Cook. (Heinemann, 10s. 6d.)

The following Board of Education publications (H.M.S.O.) should be studied:

The Teaching of English. (1921; 1s. 6d.)
Some Suggestions for the Teaching of English in Secondary Schools. (1924; 1s.)
The Education of the Adolescent. (1926; 2s.)

Books in Public Elementary Schools. (1928; 1s. 3d.)
The Primary School. (1931; 2s. 6d.)
Handbook of Suggestions for the Consideration of Teachers in Public Elementary Schools. (2s.)

Speech Training

The Play Way of Speech Training. R. Bennett. (Evans, 3s. 6d.)
The Pronunciation of English. D. Jones. (Cambridge, 4s.)

The Writing of English

The Writing of English. W. T. Brewster. (Butterworth, 2s. 6d.)
The Art of Writing. Sir A. T. Quiller-Couch. (Cambridge, 5s.)
Modern English Usage. H. W. Fowler. (Oxford, 7s. 6d.)
The King's English. H. W. and F. G. Fowler. (Oxford, 6s.)
Matter, Form and Style. H. O'Grady. (Murray, 3s.)

The Language

The English Language. L. Pearsall Smith. (Butterworth, 2s. 6d.)
Growth and Structure of the English Language. Otto Jespersen. (Blackwell, 6s.)
Elementary Lessons in English Grammar. H. C. K. Wyld. (Oxford, 2s. 6d.)
Report of Joint Committee on Grammatical Terminology. (Murray, 1s.)

Literature

A History of English Literature. Edited by John Buchan. (Nelson, 10s. 6d.)

Verse

Lessons in Verse-Craft. S. Gertrude Ford. (Daniel, 3s. 6d.)
The Discovery of Poetry. P. H. B. Lyon. (Arnold, 2s. 6d.)
The Speaking of English Verse. Elsie Fogerty. (Dent, 6s.)

But let the teacher take courage. First let him read a passage 'at the long breath'—as the French say—aloud, and persuasively as he can. Now and then he may pause to indicate some particular beauty, repeating the line before he proceeds. But he should be sparing of such interruptions. When Laughter, for example, is already 'holding both his sides' it cannot be less than officious, a work of supererogation, to stop and hold them for him; and he who obeys the counsel of perfection will read straight to the end and then recur to particular beauties. Next let him put up a child to continue with the tale, and another and another, just as in a construing class. While the boy is reading, the teacher should *never* interrupt: he should wait, and return afterwards upon a line that has been slurred or wrongly emphasised. When the children have done reading he should invite questions on any point they have found puzzling: it is with the operation of poetry on *their* minds that his main business lies. Lastly, he may run back over significant points they have missed.

'And is this all the method?'—Yes, that is all the method. 'So simple as that?'—Yes, even so simple as that, and (I claim) even so wise, seeing that it just lets the author— Chaucer or Shakespeare or Milton or Coleridge—have his own way with the young plant—just lets them drop 'like the gentle rain from heaven', and soak in....For the quality of Poetry is not strained. Let the rain soak; then use your hoe, and gently; and still trust Nature; by which, I again repeat to you, all spirit attracts all spirit as inevitably as all matter attracts all matter.

SIR ARTHUR QUILLER-COUCH, *On the Art of Reading*

INDEX TO CHIEF TOPICS

(Roman figures refer to Stages)

Printed in the United States
by Bookmasters

Printed in the United States
By Bookmasters